Creative Card Design: Promotional Greetings

PIE BOOKS

Creative Card Design: Promotional Greetings

Copyright ©2008 PIE BOOKS

All right reserved. No part of this publication may be reproduced in any form or by any means, graphic, electronic or mechanical, including photocopying and recording by an information storage and retrieval system, without permission in writing from the publisher.

PIE BOOKS
2-32-4, Minami-Otsuka, Toshima-ku, Tokyo 170-0005 JAPAN
Phone: +81-3-5395-4811 Fax: +81-3-5395-4812
e-mail: editor@piebooks.com   sales@piebooks.com
http://www.piebooks.com

ISBN978-4-89444-677-9 C3070

Printed in Japan

CONTENTS

Foreword 004-007
Promotion 009-048
Invitations 049-098
Greetings 099-132
Others 133-152
Index 153-157

Creative Card Design: Promotional Greetings

はじめに

ダイレクトメールは、長い間、広告媒体の一つとして確固たる位置を占めてきましたが、ここ数年、デジタルメディアなどの台頭により、発送数は減少傾向にあります。

しかしながら、ここにきて変化の兆しがあらわれています。
インターネットでのネットサーフィン、際限のないスパムメール、そしてTVでのマルチチャンネル化などによって情報が氾濫し、本当に必要な情報だけを発信することも、受け取ることも難しくなっています。そのため、必要な情報を必要な相手へ届けるための手段としてDMというメディアが見直されているのです。

近年、よりセグメントされた顧客に対して、訴求力（パワー）のあるDMが増えてきたことからも明らかです。

本書では、受け手のアクション（行動喚起）につながっていく、言い換えれば、レスポンス率の高いDMで、特に色や形、素材などに工夫がなされている作品を世界中から集めています。
皆さまが、そのパワフルなメッセージ訴求力を持った作品から、今後のDM制作へのインスピレーションを得られましたら幸いです。

最後になりますが、忙しいなかご協力いただき、快く作品をご提供いただいたクリエイターの皆さまにこの場を借りてお礼を申し上げます。

PIE BOOKS 編集部

Creative Card Design: Promotional Greetings

Foreword

For many years direct mail has been an important medium for the advertising and public relations industry. However, in the past few years, as a result of the rise of digital and other new types of media, the volume of direct mail being sent out has decreased.

Nevertheless, there are indications that things are changing.

With the surfeit of information produced by internet surfing, endless volumes of spam, and the profusion of television channels, it has become very difficult for people to dispatch or receive only that information which they feel is necessary. Consequently, direct mail has been reevaluated as an effective means of communicating necessary information to specific people.

It is clear that the appeal of direct mail is increasing for a public that is becoming more and more segmented.

This book presents examples of direct mail from all over the world, including ideas that provoke actions from recipients – in other words, a high response rate – as well as direct mail that utilizes clever concepts involving special colors, shapes, and materials. It would be very gratifying to know that readers can derive inspiration for future direct mail productions from these examples, which demonstrate a very powerful appeal.

We would like to express our appreciation to all the creators who took time out of their busy schedules to submit examples of their work for this book.

PIE BOOKS

EDITORIAL NOTES

A
カテゴリー
Category

B
デザインコンセプト
Design Concept

C
スタッフクレジット
Staff Credits

CL: Client / Brand name　クライアント／ブランド名
CD: Creative Director　クリエイティブ・ディレクター
AD: Art Director　アート・ディレクター
D: Designer　デザイナー
P: Photographer　カメラマン
I: Illustrator　イラストレーター
CW: Copywriter　コピーライター
DF: Design Firm　デザイン事務所
S: Submittor　作品提供者

* 上記以外の制作者呼称は、省略せずに記載しています。
Full names of all others involved in the creation / production of the work.

* 広告作品に掲載されているセールやキャンペーン情報は、すでに終了しております。ご了承ください。
Please be aware that sales and campaign information in the ads shown within are no longer valid.

* 提供者の意向により、クレジットデータの一部を記載していないものがあります。
Some credit data has been omitted at the contributor's request.

* 本書に記載された企業名・商品名は、掲載各社の商標または登録商標です。
The company and product names that appear in this book are published and /or registered trademarks.

Promotion

Promotion

Promotional holiday gift with a lighting theme
The theme is festive lights, a fixture of the holiday season that expresses the joy of gift-giving. The purpose of the gift is to make customers not directly involved in the creative field experience the joy of creation by assembling something themselves.

明かりをテーマにした、デザイン会社のPR用ホリデーギフト
ホリデーシーズンに付き物の「明かり」がテーマ。「喜び」や「贈る気持ち」を表現している。自分で組み立てることにより、クリエイティブに直接関係のない業界の顧客にも、ものづくりを体感してもらうことを狙った。

CL, DF, S: Real Art Design Group,Inc.　CD: Chris Wire　AD: Jeremy Loyd

Promotion

Promotion

Design studio greeting gift linked to a photo contest
This gift contained a Holga camera, film, and photo album. When the film was returned after being exposed, an album full of contact sheets was made. The contest was held on the web and winners received their works framed.

写真コンテストと連動したデザイン・スタジオのカメラギフト
Holgaのカメラ、フィルム、アルバムの入ったギフト。撮影済フィルムを返送すると、このアルバムサイズのコンタクトシートにしてくれる。ウェブ上ではコンテストも行われ受賞者には額装した受賞作品が贈られた。

CL, DF, S: Real Art Design Group,Inc.　CD: Chris Wire　AD: Jeremy Loyd　D: Creative Team Group Effort

Promotion

Announcement for new showroom of appliance maker Smeg Italy
A company whose products are made in collaboration with designers sent this direct mail to designers. Shapes familiar to designers, such as color swatches, are used. The idea came from the golden age of Italian design in the 1950s and 60s. The tube packaging also stimulates curiosity.

筒状パッケージが興味を引く、家電メーカーの新ショールームへの案内状
デザイナーとのコラボ商品を生産する同社が、デザイナーを対象に配布したDM。色見本帳などデザイナーに馴染み深い形を採用。50〜60年代の黄金期の伊デザインから着想を得ている。筒状パッケージも興味を引く。

S: Fenice Pool CL: Smeg Italy

Promotion

Direct mail to promote the values of Form
This direct mail promotes the work, character, and values of the UK design company Form. The shape fits the human hand. Inside are reproductions of the company's work accompanied by comments from clients. On the back is a playful use of typography using low-key colors, expressing the philosophy of Form.

デザイン会社の仕事実例を見せる、じゃばら式DM
UKのデザイン会社Formの仕事、キャラクター、価値を伝えるためのDM。手に馴染む形を採用。中面は顧客の感想とともに仕事を紹介。裏は色目を抑えタイポグラフィーで遊び、Formの世界観を表現している。

CL, DF, S: Form　　CD, AD, D, CW: Paula Benson　　CD, AD, D: Paul West　　D, P: Andy Harvey

Promotion

Nike Pro line and Nike Warrior campaign
Before games, pro athletes prepare to compete. Just like warriors they make themselves physically and mentally ready for battle. The products embody this concept. They exert an authentic aura of courage and raw aggression.

アスリートの戦闘体勢を表現した Nike Pro / Nike Warrior キャンペーン
試合前のプロアスリートたちは、戦いに向けて準備をする。まるで戦士のように、肉体的にも精神的にも戦闘態勢に入る。そんなコンセプトを具現化した作品。勇敢でむき出しの本物感を演出した。

S: ceft and company   CL: New York,NY   CD: Ucef Hanjani   AD: Kimberley Norcott
DF: Shadi＋company / clockwork apple / The Ace group

015

Promotion

Promotion tool for Goethe-Institut
A promotion tool published to celebrate the eleven German-speaking winners of the Nobel Prize in Literature. Because the subject is literature, the format is small books in slipcases. Each book contains passages from the works of one of the writers.

ノーベル賞受賞を祝って制作したドイツの文化機関のプロモーションDM
ドイツ語を話す11人のノーベル文学賞受賞者を祝して発行されたプロモーション・ツール。文学賞にちなんで、フォーマットはケースに入った小冊子とし、それぞれ作家の作品の抜粋を掲載している。

S: Brighten the Corners   CL: Goethe-Institut   CD, AD, D: Billy Kiossoglou / Frank Philippin

Promotion

Website announcement with a reproduction of a finger
Direct mail that announces the website of a design studio. The startling finger that's enclosed is a copy of the designer's own finger, which "thinks, creates, attracts, selects, differentiates, begins, and causes."

デザイナー自身の指の複製が入った、デザイン・スタジオのウェブサイト案内
デザイン・スタジオのウェブサイトを案内するDM。衝撃的な中の「指」は、考え、創造し、魅了し、選択し、他との違いを生み出し、何かを始め、何かを起こす、デザイナー本人の指を複製したもの。

CL, CD, AD, D, DF, S: Xose Teiga

017

Promotion

Greeting for a design office that includes a real brick
A real brick was used to convey the idea of a new business at a new location as well as a new life being built up from scratch. It expresses the weight of new beginnings. The recipients were both surprised and pleased.

本物のレンガを使って起業の大変さを表現したデザイン・オフィスの挨拶状
新しい場所での新しいビジネス……新しい人生を一から積み上げていく、というイメージから本物のレンガを使用。新スタートがどれだけ「ヘビー」だったかを表現した。驚かれたと同時に大いに喜ばれた。

DF, S: DESIGN CENTER LTD.　CL, CD, D, CW: Eduard Cehovin　P: Janez Vlachy

Promotion

Direct mail for a realtor that includes a brick
The Palazzo Biscotto is a special building with a double layer structure and a brick exterior. "Bis" means double and "Cotto" means brick. Inside the direct mailing is a sample of the brick that was actually used in the construction. It can be used as a paperweight.

実際使用されたレンガのサンプルで建物の特徴を語る、不動産会社のDM
Palazzo Biscottoは、外側がレンガでできた二重構造の特殊な建物。BIS＝二重、COTTO＝レンガを意味する。中に入っているのは実際使用されたレンガのサンプルで、ペーパーウェイトにもなる。

DF, S: Raineri Design　CL: Palazzo Biscotto / Paterlini Real Estate

019

Promotion

Direct mail for building materials manufacturer that includes a brick

This promotional direct mail was aimed at architects. The box contains a set of pamphlets and a small special-order brick (numbered). Because it contains a genuine brick that the recipients can hold in their hands, the client succeeded in cultivating new customers with this direct mailing.

本物のレンガサンプルに触れられる、建築家に向けた建材メーカーのDM
建築家に向けたプロモーションDM。ボックスの中には、パンフレットとともに特注の小さなレンガ（番号付）をセット。実際にレンガに触れることのできる印象的なDMにより、新規顧客の獲得に成功した。

S: Daniela Vascellari　CL: MISTER BRICK SRL　CD: Federico Frasson

Promotion

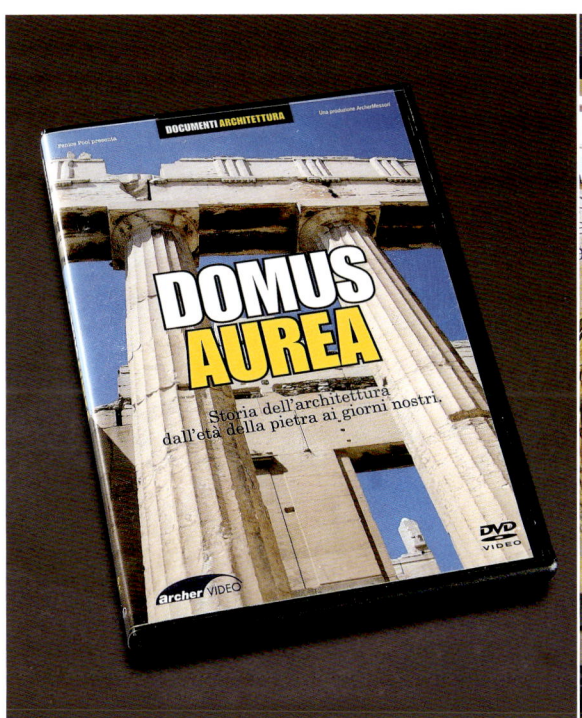
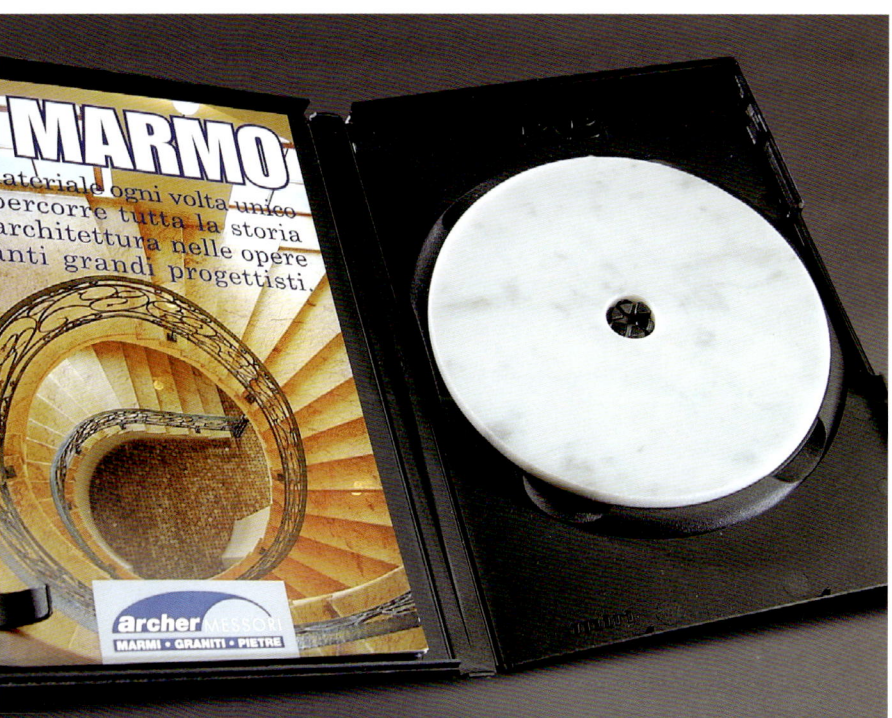

Promoting vision and technology with a marble DVD
Direct mail for a marble factory in northern Italy. On the cover of DVD cases are the words "the history of our work," and inside there is a marble disk rather than a DVD. The idea directly conveys the vision of a sculptor or architect.

DVDの形をした大理石で、大理石加工業者のビジョンと技術をアピール
イタリア北部にある大理石加工業者のDM。「これまでの仕事」と書かれたDVDパッケージの中には、DVDの代わりに大理石でできたディスクが入っており、造形作家のヴィジョンをダイレクトに伝えている。

S: Fenice Pool　CL: Archer Messori

021

Promotion

Direct mail for Nikon Big in which letters appear
This promotional direct mail introduced Nikon's Big. The recipient moves the card and letters appear. The purpose is to make people think, "I get it," with a slight sense of surprise and discovery.

伸ばすと文字が現れる、Nikon ビッグのプロモーション用DM
NikonのBIGを紹介するプロモーション用のDM。受け取った人がカードを動かすことで、文字が現れる仕組みで、小さな驚きと発見に「なるほど！」と思わせることを狙った。

DF, S: Mirko Ilic Corp   CL: Nikon   CD: Michael Mellett   AD, D: Mirko Ilic

Announcement for Motel 2004 summer collection
This direct mail announced the summer collection of the apparel brand Motel. The designer used a bound pamphlet style whose envelope is part of the pamphlet in order to present several different brands using one promotional material.

アパレルブランド Motel のサマーコレクションのお知らせ
アパレルブランドMotelの夏のコレクションの告知DM。数ブランドの情報をひとつにまとめるための手法として、封筒と合体した中綴じパンフレットの形状を採用した。

CD, AD, D, S: Nesco   DF: Nigrec Design   CL: Motel Inc.

Promotion

Direct mail for enhancing image of a bioengineering equipment company
Since research into waves is central to this company's mission of developing biotech equipment, a three-dimensional rendering of a wave motif was used. It promotes the idea that the company is engaged in technological innovation from a creative standpoint and distinguishes the company from others of its kind.

波動をモチーフにしたDMで、生体工学機器メーカーのイメージUPを図る
「波動」の研究が同社の機器開発において重要な鍵となってきたことから、波をモチーフにした立体的なオブジェを採用。クリエイティブな発想で技術革新を行う企業であることをアピールし、差別化を図った。

DF, S: Heinz Wild Design   CL: Bioengineering AG   CD, AD, D: Heinz Wild   D: Dan Petter
P: Michael Rast / St.Gallen   CW: Kurt Schori / Gabriella Meyer

Promotion

Promotional direct mail for a bioengineering equipment manufacturer
This toy represents the concept of gravity and only works when you know the trick to it. The box contains a mathematical explanation. It expresses the company's "unique concepts," "creative thinking," and "simple but amazing ideas."

生体工学機器メーカーの創造性をアピールする、重力をテーマとしたおもちゃ
トリックが分からないと遊べない、重力をテーマとしたおもちゃ。箱の中には、数学的な解説が入っている。同社の「ユニークな発想」「クリエイティブな考え方」「シンプルながら驚くべきアイデア」を表している。

DF, S: Heinz Wild Design CL: Bioengineering AG CD, AD, D, I: Heinz Wild D: Dan Petter
CW: Christian Wissler / Erich Kastner Translation: Erich Brandenberger

025

Promotion

Spring greeting gift for bioengineering equipment manufacturer
This chocolate gift came with an explanation about a precision-made valve. Ideally, after the chocolate is eaten the container is retained, thus reminding the recipient of the company that sent it. The tin container used for the packaging can be reused for other things.

生体工学機器メーカーが送る、精密機械のバルブ型チョコレート・ギフト
精密機械のバルブに関する説明が同封されたチョコレート・ギフト。食べ終わった後も捨てられることなく、いつまでも同社のことを思い出してもらうことを狙って、パッケージは入れ物として使えるブリキ缶とした。

DF, S: Heinz Wild Design   CL: Bioengineering AG   CD, AD, D, I, CW: Heinz Wild   P: Michael Rast
CW: Joachim Ringelnatz   Translation: Erich Brandenberger

Promotion

Wave-shaped direct mail expressing the talents of a model maker
The client, Rene Scherr, is a leading model maker. The material used was wave-shaped cardboard and the logo was embossed by hand. The direct mail was made to convey the client's special traits.

模型制作家の専門性を伝える波型ダイレクトメール
依頼主であるRENE SCHERRは模型制作の専門家。素材には波型の板紙を使い、ロゴは手作業によるエンボス加工を施した。依頼主の専門性を伝えるDMに仕上がった。

DF, S: SAGENVIER DESIGNKOMMUNIKATION   CL: RENE SCHERR   CD, AD: Sigi Ramoser
D: Marcel Schrattner

Promotion

Publicity direct mail for a charitable organization
A direct mailing for a non-profit organization that works with victims of domestic violence. It alerts people to the idea that scars which result from domestic violence are deep and take time to heal.

破れによって家庭内暴力の傷を表現した、慈善団体の広報用DM
家庭内暴力に苦しむ人々を支援する非営利団体のダイレクト・メール。家庭内暴力が被害者に残す傷は深く、すぐには消えないということを表現し、人々の関心を喚起している。

DF, S: Kinetic Singapore   CL: Pave   CD, AD, D: Pann Lim   CD, AD: Roy Poh   P: Jeremy Wong

028

Promotion

Announcement for a new line of products from an electric appliance maker.

This announcement notified retail buyers of the availability of the new V. Smile Baby line from Vtech. Prior to sending out boxes of chocolate cigars to announce that the new toy had been put on sale, the company sent out cards with a sonogram of the new arrival stating that the product would soon be born.

家電メーカーの新おもちゃシリーズ（V.Smile Baby）の案内
Vtechの新シリーズV. Smile Babyの発売をバイヤーに知らせる案内。新しいおもちゃの発売を知らせるチョコレート・シガーボックスを送付した直後に、超音波画像付きの「もうすぐ生まれます」カードが送られた。

DF, S: Real Art Design Group,Inc.　　CL: VTech Electronics　　CD: Chris Wire　　AD: Jeremy Loyd
D: Jenn Gobrail

029

Promotion

Paper craft direct mail for the brand Pedrho
Promotion card for Pedrho, an Italy-based creative visual project and the collective endeavor of artists who share a passion for prints, design, t-shirts and animals. It's a paper-craft kit for making a dog, which is considered man's best friend.

犬をテーマにTシャツを展開するブランド Pedrho の紙工作DM
グラフィック、Tシャツ、動物をテーマにプロジェクトを展開しているイタリアのクリエイティブ集団PedrhoのDM。人間の友達として人気の高い「犬」をテーマに、切り取って組み立てられる紙工作キットとした。

DF, S: Happycentro+Sintetik　CL: Pedrho　CD, AD, D, I: Federico Galvani

Promotion

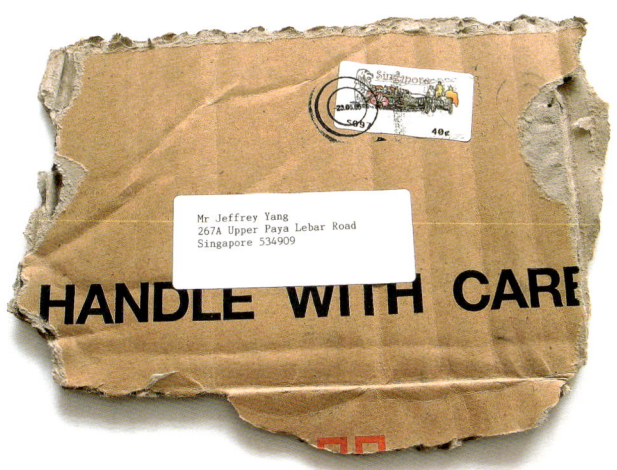

Eco-conscious website announcement for antique furniture store
Lorgan's is an interior store in Singapore that sells and repairs antique furniture and imported sundries. This direct mail notifies recipients of the store's website by recycling cardboard that was originally used for packing furniture.

アンティーク・インテリアショップの、エコを意識したウェブサイト案内
ローガンズは、シンガポールにあるアンティーク家具・雑貨の輸入・修復・販売を行っているインテリアショップ。これは店のウェブサイトを知らせるためのDMで、家具が梱包されていた段ボールを再利用している。

DF, S: Kinetic Singapore   CL: Lorgan's The Retro Store   CD, AD, D: Pann Lim   CD, AD: Roy Poh

Promotion

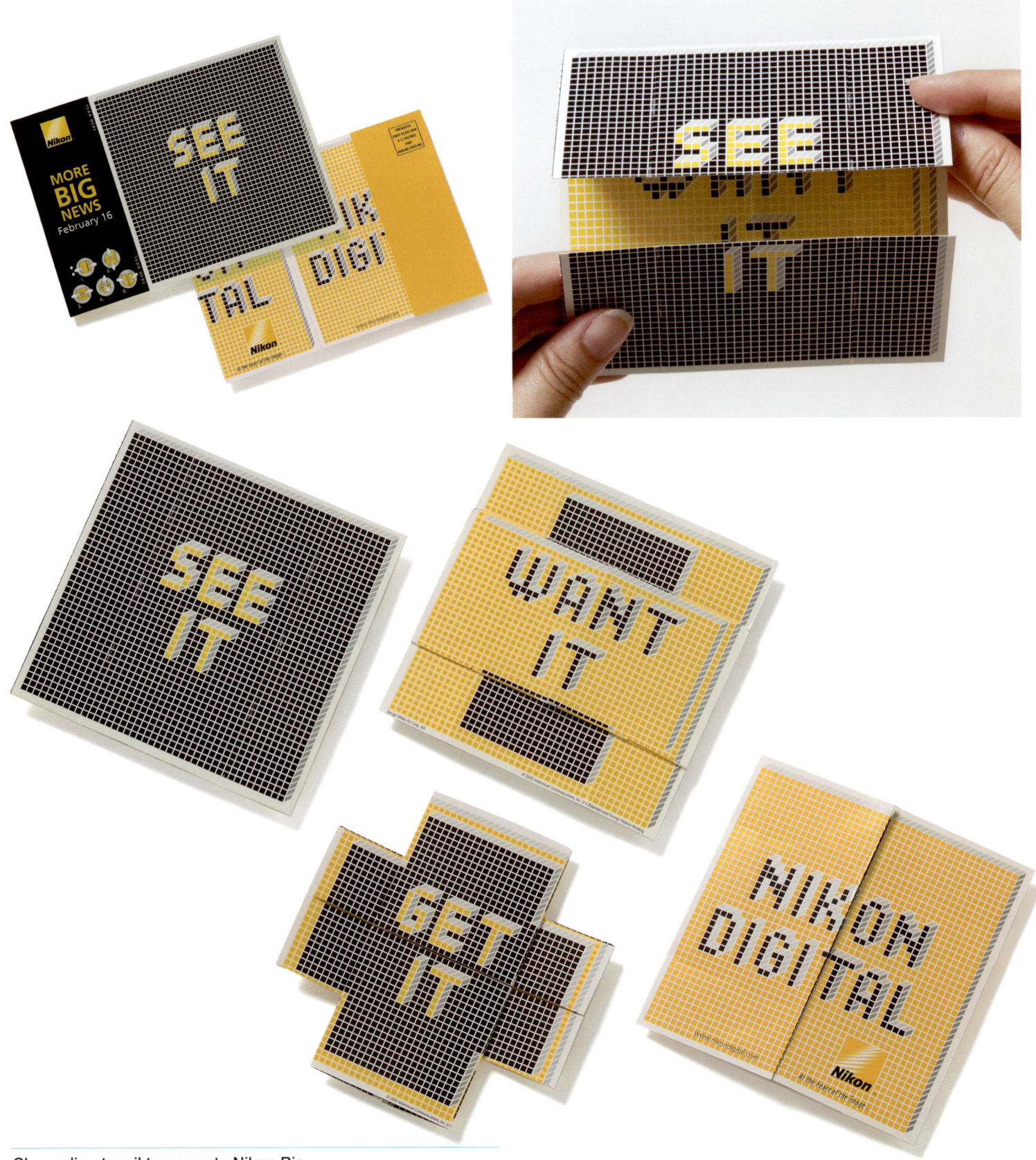

Clever direct mail to promote Nikon Big
Interactive teaser direct mail that piques the curiosity of the recipient. Various words are formed by combinations of squares when the left edge is cut off.

展開すると4つのメッセージが現れる、ニコンBIGの販促用カラクリDM
受け取った人の興味を掻き立てるインタラクティブなティーザーDM。左端を切り取り、正方形の部分を展開していくと、さまざまな言葉が現れる仕組みになっている。

DF, S: Mirko Ilic Corp   CL: Nikon   CD: Michael Mellett   AD, D: Mirko Ilic

Promotion

1
Playing card-style promotional direct mail to express a variety of services

This is a direct mail for that's nice, which is involved in branding and marketing. Illustrations and nicknames describe the special character of the staff, as well as the breadth of the work the company performs. The cards come in a custom made tin box. They are also linked to an online card game.

スタッフをキャラクター化し事業の多様性を表した、デザイン会社のトランプ

ブランディング、マーケティングを手がけるthat's niceのDM。イラストとニックネームでスタッフの特徴を描き、仕事の幅広さを表現。特製のブリキボックス入り。オンラインカードゲームとも連動している。

DF, S: That's Nice LLC　Managing Director: Nigel Walker

2
Novelty to commemorate the opening of an outdoor select shop

The designer received a request from a shop owner who wanted to distribute a carbina (key holder). The designer's solution was to produce a simple package using color copies and home-use vacuum packing equipment.

アウトドア・セレクトショップのオープン記念ノベルティ

ショップオーナーからカルビナ(キーホルダー)を配りたいとの依頼があり、デザインソリューションとして、カラーコピーと家庭用真空パック機を使用してシンプルなパッケージを制作した。

CD, AD, D, DF, S: Fukuda Kenji Graphic Design　　CL: UTILITY

1
Wine gift with investment information printed on the bottle
This promotion tool targeted investors for Intercell, a bioengineering company in Austria. Detailed information about Intercell's business model was silk-screened on a bottle.

投資家向けの情報を直接ボトルに印刷した、バイオ企業のワインギフト
オーストリアのバイオテクノロジー企業Intercellの投資家を対象としたプロモーション。インターセルのビジネスモデルに関する詳細が、ボトルにスクリーン印刷されている。

DF, S: alessandridesign　CL: INTERCELL AG　CD: Cordula Alessandri　AD: Hans Proschofsky
CW: Cosima Reif

2
Promotional direct mail for men from a barber
This direct mail was sent out barbers. When the envelope is opened it turns into a mirror. The recipient can then check his own hairstyle. The paper used for the envelope is Specialties No. 312.

鏡で髪をチェックできる、男性向け理容室のプロモーションDM
理容室を告知するためのDM。封筒を開けると髭の模様の入った鏡になっており、受け取った人が顔を鏡に合わせることで、自分の髪をチェックできるようになっている。封筒に使用した用紙はスペシャリティーズNo.312。

DF, S: KURI-LAB.　CL: Executive Men's Salon DONFUN　CD: Hiro Koike　AD, D: Koji Kurihara
Producer: Takuya Yamakawa　CW: Eiichiro Hirayama

Promotion

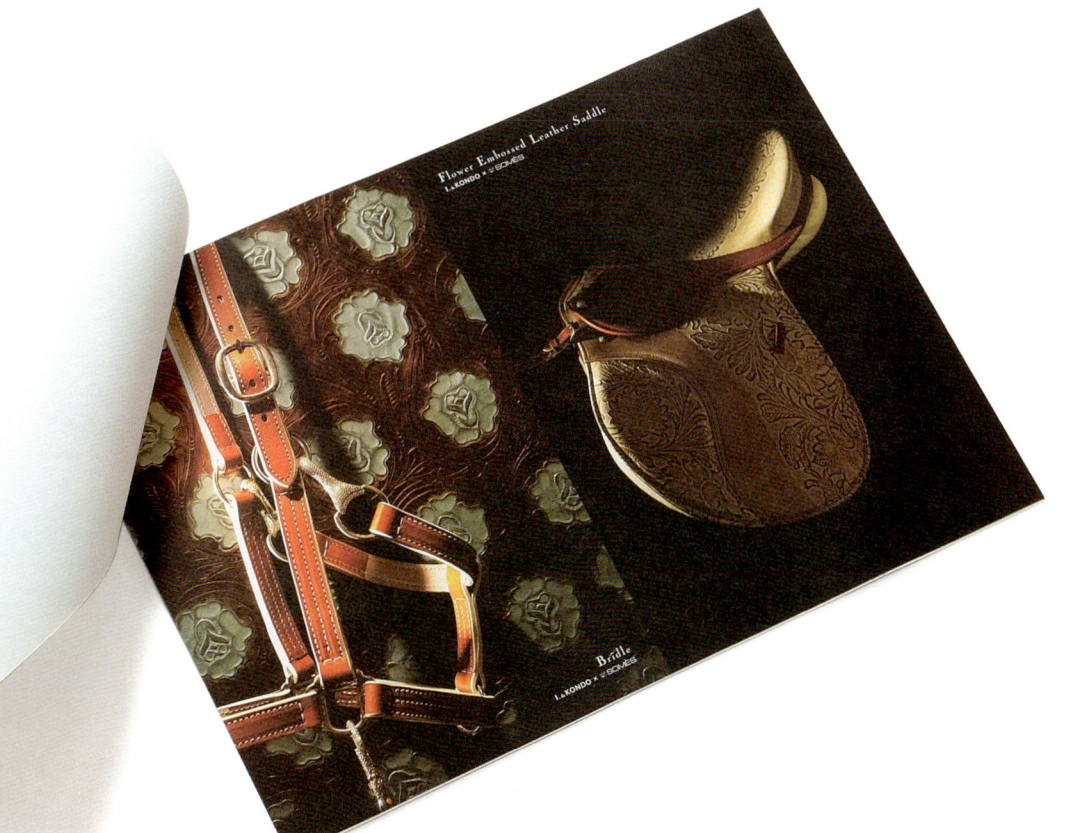

Collection catalogue for L & Kondo
A leather lifestyle collection catalogue centered on the theme of Dubai. The point of the design is leather parts. The materials used were leather, Studs and paper.

レザーブランド、ルコンドのドバイをテーマにしたコレクションのカタログ
Dubaiをテーマとしたレザーライフスタイル・コレクション・カタログ。デザインのポイントはレザーパーツ。素材には革、カシメ、紙を使用している。

S: STUDIO DESIGN·K CO.,LTD.　CL: L & KONDO　CD: Kaneyoshi Kondo　AD: Hiroaki Nagai
P: Eriko Sakihama　DF: NG CO.,LTD.

035

Promotion

Old-fashioned product announcement for an antique store
This direct mail introduces the new merchandise of an antique store. The concept is based on the idea of "a letter mailed in the 70s that arrived late." This retro DM provides information about used furniture that was made in the 70s but still retains its appeal.

過去の手紙かと錯覚させる、アンティーク・インテリアショップの商品案内
アンティーク・インテリアショップの新商品を紹介するDM。コンセプトは「遅延配送されてきた70年代の手紙」。レトロなDMには、時代に流されない魅力をもつ70年代の中古家具が紹介されている。

DF, S: Kinetic Singapore   CL: Lorgan's The Retro Store   CD, AD, D: Roy Poh   CD, AD: Pann Lim

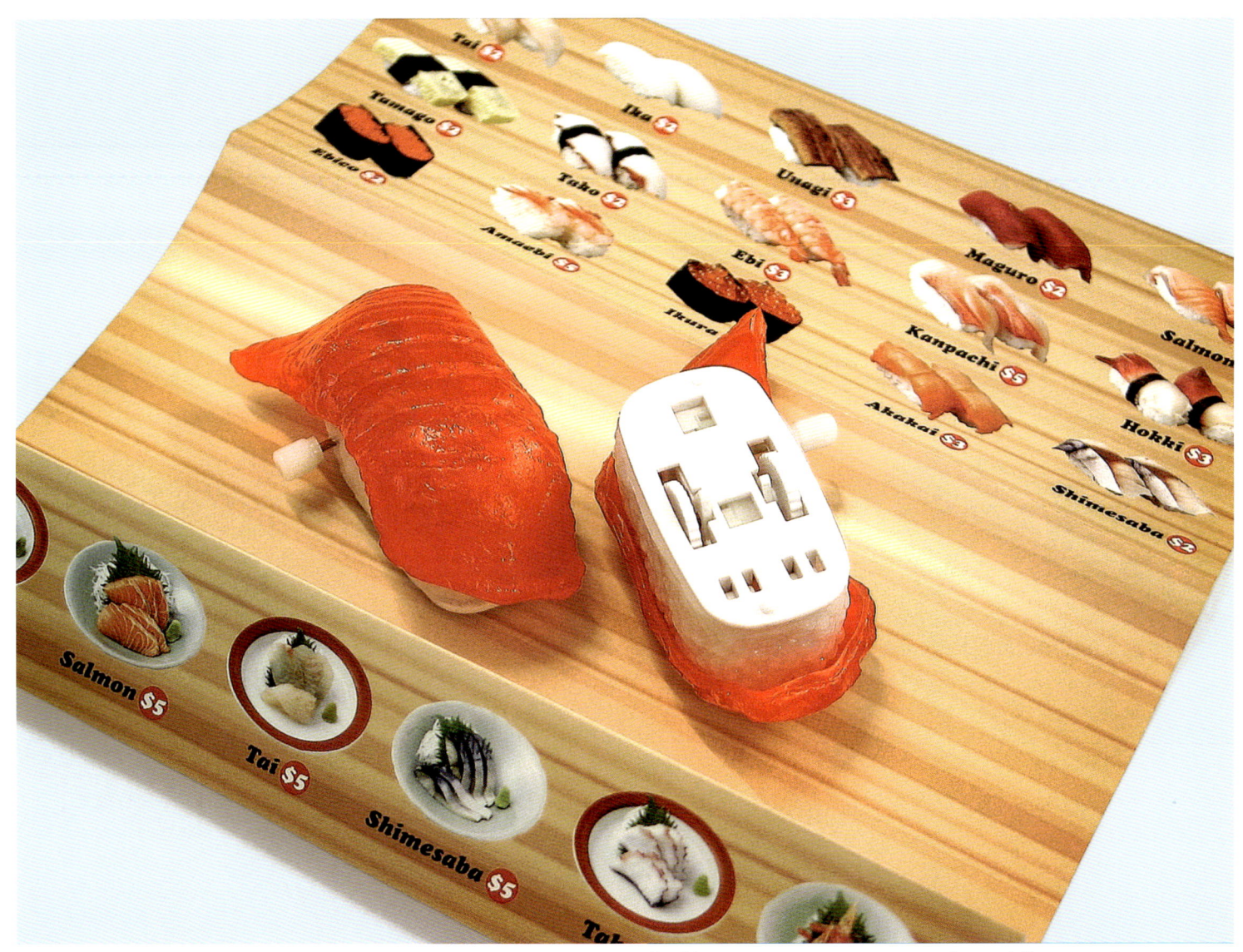

Promotion

Sushi restaurant announcement of new delivery service
This direct mail is in the form of a wind-up toy sushi and menu. The DM is distributed to office and residential districts around the Valley Point Shopping Center, where the client restaurant is located, for the purpose of announcing a new delivery service.

ぜんまい仕掛けのにぎりがキッチュな、寿司店のデリバリーサービス開始案内
ぜんまい仕掛けの寿司のおもちゃとメニューの入ったDM。デリバリーサービス開始を知らせる目的で、依頼主の店舗があるヴァレー・ポイント・ショッピングセンター周辺のオフィス街、住宅街に配布された。

DF, S: Kinetic Singapore CL: Nagano Sushi CD, AD, D: Roy Poh CD, AD: Pann Lim

Promotion

Beauty salon promotion-cum-shop card that people remember
An eyeglass form was used for the purpose of provoking the desire for change that everyone has, but recipients also enjoyed wearing them, which means they will remember them. 1c/1c + die-cut processing was used so the cost was low. They were very popular and after being distributed in nearby cafes quickly disappeared.

記憶に残ることを狙った美容院のプロモーション（ショップカード兼用）
誰もがもつ変身願望をくすぐるメガネ型を採用。装着して楽しんでもらい、記憶に残すことを重要視した。1c／1c＋型抜き加工だけで低コストを実現している。人気があり、近隣のカフェ等に置くと、すぐになくなった。

S: Fuji-san Graphics　　CL: SHAMAN hair　　AD, D, CW: Hiroshi Kawamoto

Promotion

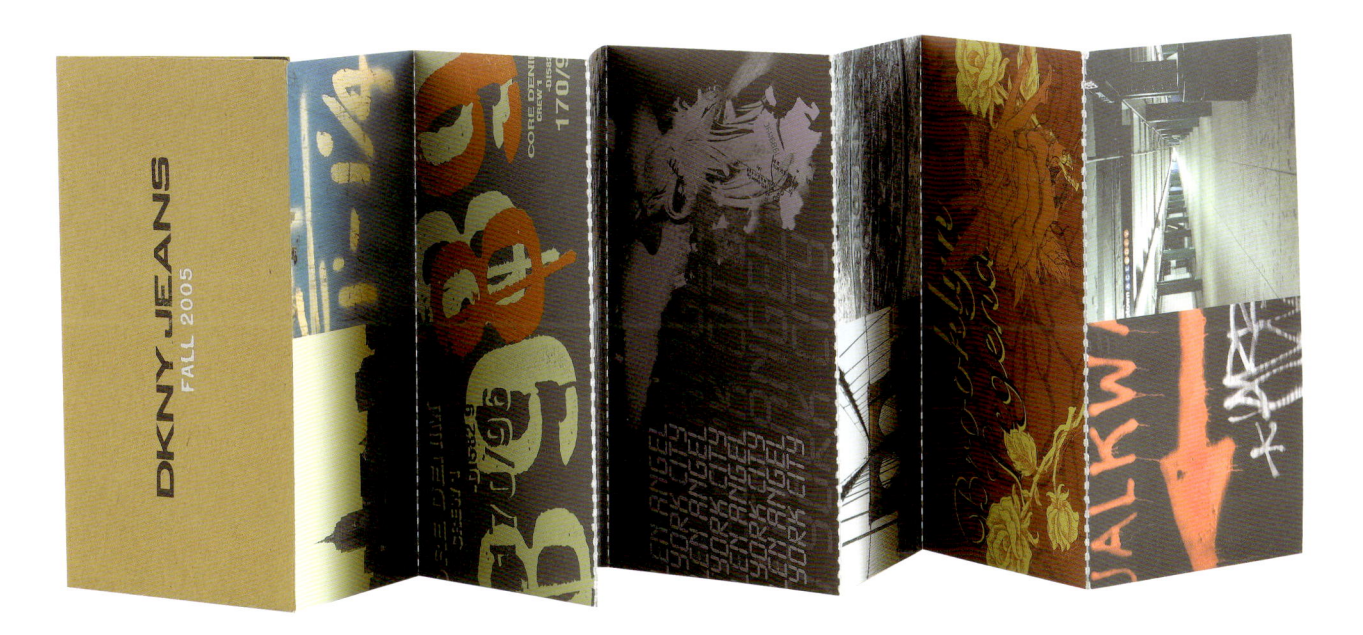

1

Announcement of the fall collection presentation for DKNY Jeans
This invitation is based on the theme of New York City. It is a set of postcards, with photographs of New York alternating with prints of the collection to be exhibited.

ファッションブランド DKNY Jeans の秋コレクション発表会の告知
ニューヨークの街をテーマにしたインビテーション・カード。ポストカードになっていて、ニューヨークの写真と、展示されるコレクションの絵柄が交互にレイアウトされている。

DF, S: Joseph Rossi srl　CL: DKNY　D: Graphic First Aid

Annual summertime greeting cards
These cards take advantage of the texture of newsprint and the feeling one gets when opening a full-scale newspaper. Medium-weight paper is used to create a retro mood. The recipes for the cocktails used in the photograph are original, so some of the recipients actually brought them to a bar and asked the bartender to concoct them.

デザイン会社が送る、ニュースペーパー感覚の暑中見舞い
ニュースペーパー感覚と、広げるスケール感を訴求。レトロな雰囲気を演出する中質紙を使用。撮影したカクテルのレシピもオリジナルで開発したもので、中には行きつけのバーで作ってもらったという人もいた。

DF, S: Tidbit Co.,Ltd.　CD, AD, CW: Masayuki Watanabe　D: Takaya Ito　P: Masaru Honda

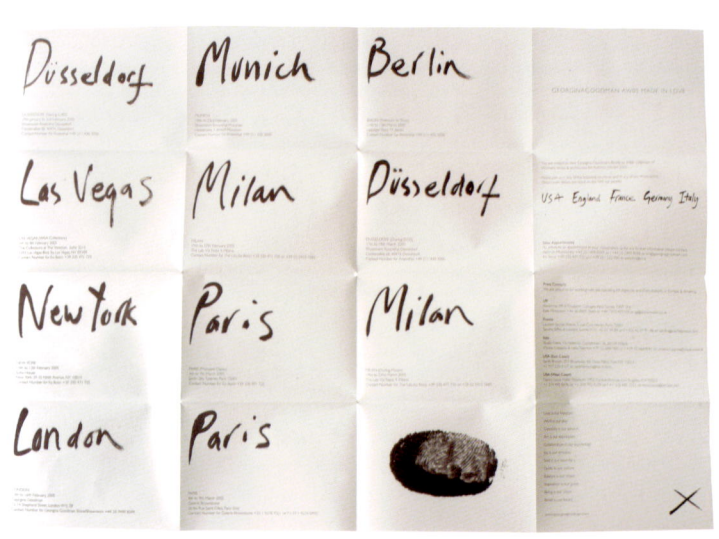

Promotion

Promotional tools for shoe designer Georgina Goodman
These promotional tools are produced annually for press and buyers all over the world. The designer chooses the shape, paper, and process in order to express the imagination and originality that's characteristic of the brand. The invitations, style books, and catalogues all reflect the theme of each collection.

各コレクションのテーマを反映した、靴デザイナーの個性的なDM
世界のプレスとバイヤーに向けて毎年制作しているツール。このブランドの幻想的で美しい個性を表現できるような形状、用紙、加工を選択。招待状、スタイルブック、カタログは各コレクションのテーマを反映している。

DF, S: Aloof Design   CL: Georgina Goodman   CD: Sam Aloof   D: Chris Barham / Andrew Scrase

Promotion

Notice for a new season collection
In order to take advantage of the unique world of Dusan Reljin, a New York-based fashion photographer, the notice provides impact by using UV embossing and graded typography. The black background contrasts with the four-color printing and high gloss to convey sophistication.

アパレルブランド UNTITLED の新シリーズ・コレクションの案内
NYのファッション・フォトグラファーDusan Reljinの独特な世界観を生かすため、タイポグラフィもグラデーションとし、UV厚盛加工でインパクトをつけた。地の黒も4c＋グロスニスで引き締め、高級感を出している。

DF, S: DESIGN BOY Inc.　CL: WORLD CO.,LTD.　CD: Kazufumi Nagai　AD, D: Shin Orishige
CW: Takako Sasaki / Naoko Gomi / Mayu Onishi　P: Dusan Reljin

Promotion

Announcement for apparel brands that take advantage of paper texture, printing and processing
This direct mail announcement was for the 2008 spring-summer sample rental for kiminori morishita, HALB, and TÊTE HOMME. Typography was printed on cushiony thick paper cut into a large, round shape in order to create an impact with only the printing material.

紙の風合いと印刷・加工を生かしたアパレル・ブランドの案内状
kiminori morishita、HALB、TÊTE HOMMEの08年春夏サンプル貸し出し案内のDM。大きめの円形にクッション性のある厚紙を使用して活版印刷と箔押しを施し、印刷物ならではの質感によりインパクトを出した。

AD, D, DF, S: Hiromi Fujita   CL: TÊTE HOMME CO.,LTD.

042

Promotion

Promotional direct mail that catches the eye the moment it arrives
This is a direct mail catalogue for the Lifestyle Curator Service of members salon CELUX. Overall impact, including the package, is stressed when the catalogue is delivered. Vinyl and paper were used.

届いた瞬間から目を引く、会員制サロンCELUXのカタログDM
会員制サロンCELUXのサービスのひとつ「Lifestyle Curator Service」のカタログDM。パッケージまで含めて、届いたときのインパクトを重視した。素材はビニールと紙を使用。

DF, S: CAP Inc.　CL: CELUX COMPANY LVJ GROUP K.K.　AD: Yasushi Fujimoto　D: Hiromi Fujita

043

Notice for new season collection
Making the most of the natural, clean world of Vanina Sorrenti, a New York-based fashion photographer, in order to take advantage of the attractive white paper titles and illustrations are embossed for a sophisticated look.

アパレルブランド UNTITLED の新シリーズ・コレクションの告知
NYで活躍するファッション・フォトグラファーVanina Sorrentiのナチュラルでクリーンな世界観を生かした。紙白の美しさを生かすため、タイトルやイラストはエンボス加工とし、上品な仕上がりに。

DF, S: DESIGN BOY Inc.　CL: WORLD CO.,LTD.　CD: Kazufumi Nagai　AD, D: Shin Orishige
CW: Takako Sasaki / Naoko Gomi / Mayu Onishi　P: Vanina Sorrenti　I: Noriko Okaku

Promotion

Tın Tab

A unique design and manufacturing company with a highly considered approach to detail and an in-depth understanding of materials.

Disciplines include:

Staircases

Furniture

Kitchens

Buildings

Multi-Ply specialist materials

Pamphlet-cum-direct mail for interior brand
Eight-page pamphlet (direct mail) distributed at exhibitions as a promotional tool for staircases designed and produced by Tin Tab. The three-dimensional staircase was created using die cutting and machined holes on a single sheet of paper.

インテリア・ブランドが設計した「階段」をPRするパンフレットDM
Tin Tabが設計・製作した「階段」の販促ツールとして、展示会で配布された8p パンフレット（DM）。3Dの階段は、1枚の紙から、ダイカットとミシン目だけを用いて形づくられている。

DF, S: Aloof Design　CL: Tin Tab　CD: Sam Aloof　D: Andrew Scrase　P: Leigh Simpson

Promotion

Corporate guide and report in package form
When the item is removed from its envelope it expands like a jack-in-the-box. Various POP and photos showing how the package is used spring out, clearly expressing the company's specialty. This direct mail conveys the company's talent for suprising promotional kits.

POPやパッケージを得意とする印刷会社の仕事実例が飛び出す会社案内
封筒から取り出すとびっくり箱のように広がり、中から色々なPOPやパッケージの実例写真が飛び出す仕掛け。得意分野を明確に打ち出し、アッと驚く販促物を提案する会社であることをアピールするDM。

S: Links Co.,Ltd.　D: Chie Imori

046

Promotion

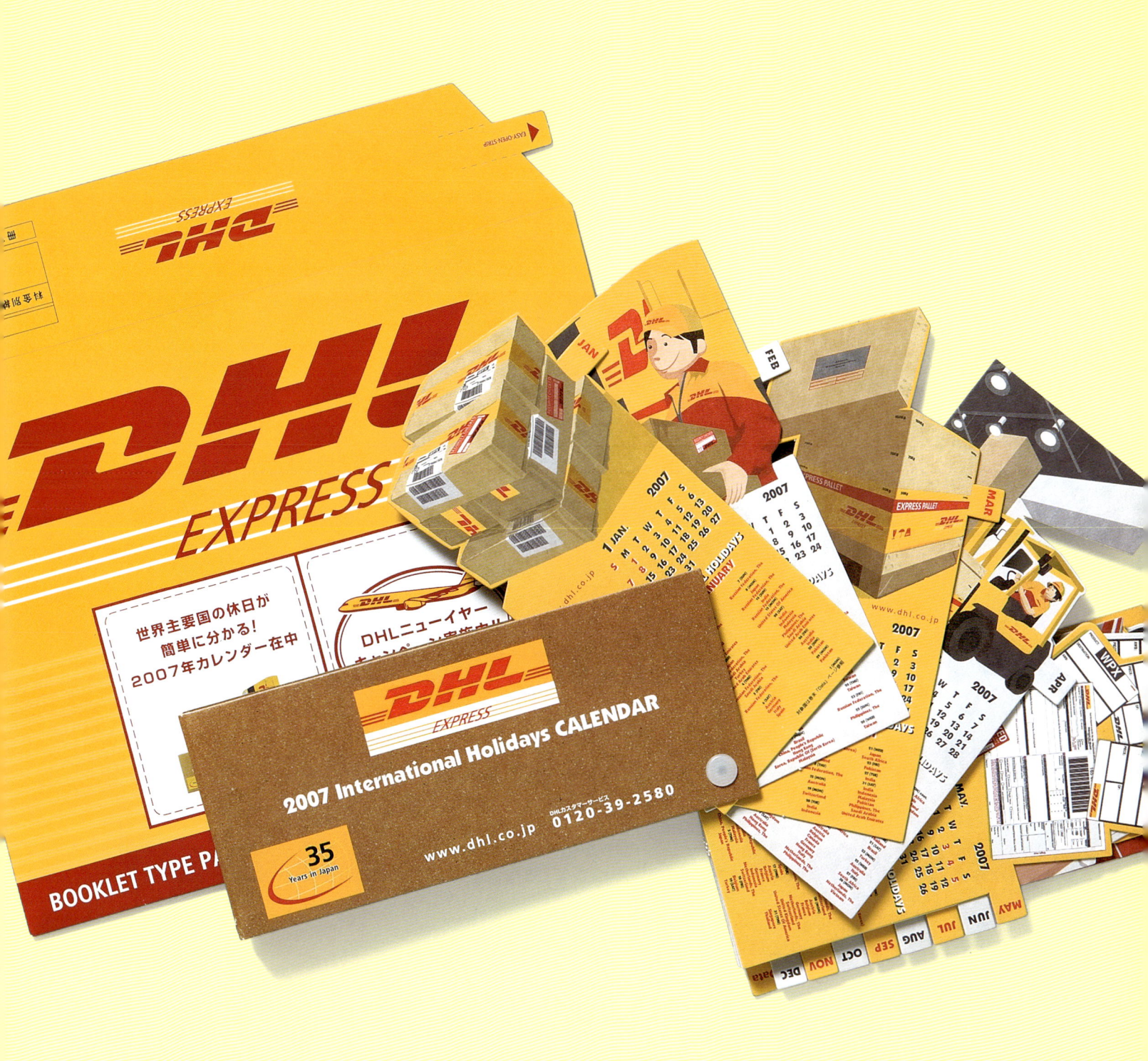

Direct mail for New Years campaign
This is for a campaign to cultivate closer relations with customers who don't employ representative salespeople. There are 12 slides-6 sets of two-that show packing materials and scenes that incorporate packing materials. The client requested that a list of world holidays be included. It was very well received.

運送会社DHLが送る、ニューイヤー・キャンペーンのカレンダー
担当営業のつかない顧客に親しみを抱いてもらうことを狙ったキャンペーン。梱包資材とそれらがある場面を2枚1組×6=12枚のスライドに。顧客からのリクエストにより掲載した世界の祝祭日の一覧が好評だった。

CL, S: DHL Japan

Promotion

1
Promotional direct mail with ink that turns white when touched
The aim was to convey a "Nordic" attention to detail even in the world of investment funds. The concept is to lend a Nordic quality to everything they touch. The blue theme color, which turns white when touched, was printed with special ink.

触ると白くなるインクを採用した北欧の金融グループのプロモーションDM
投資ファンドの世界においても細部へのこだわりを忘れない「北欧らしさ」を伝えることを狙った。「触れたものすべてに北欧らしさを残す」がコンセプト。テーマカラーの青は触ると白くなる特殊インクで印刷している。

S: room corporation   CL: nordea   CD: Paolo Prossen

2
Promotional tool to instantly convey a certain idea
This PR tool is for a school where students learn to be professional cheese makers and salespeople. The witty stationery instantly conveys the associated product and its country of origin. The holes one usually finds in cheese were represented by cut-out holes in the paper. As a result, enrollment was twice as much as originally expected.

コンセプトを一瞬で伝える、チーズの学校のプロモーション・ツール
ニュージーランドのチーズ製造販売のプロを育てる学校のPRツール。製品と原産国がひと目で伝わるユーモアたっぷりのステーショナリー。チーズの穴は型抜きで表現している。結果、入学者数が予想の2倍となった。

DF, S: The Creative Method   CL: The New Zealand Cheese School   CD, D, P: Tony Ibbotson

Invitation

Invitations

Invitation to the opening of an Italian-Japanese fusion restaurant
The card is for press people: chopsticks, knife, and fork are attached to the card to convey the idea that the restaurant specializes in fusion cuisine, a combination of Italian and Japanese cooking. In the invitation for general guests, information about the event was directly printed on a pair of chopsticks.

イタリアンと和を融合したフュージョンレストラン開店パーティーの招待状
報道関係者用のカードには箸、フォーク、ナイフが取り付けられ、イタリア料理と日本料理を融合させたフュージョン・レストランであることを表現。一般向けのものには、パーティーの情報が箸に直接印刷されている。

DF, S: Cacao Design   CL: QOR   CD: Mauro Pastore / Masa Magnoni / Alessandro Floridia
D: Giulia Landini

Invitations

Reception announcement for a robata-style Korean restaurant
Korean grill-table restaurant Ifuu is a new kind of eatery that serves Korean food in a Japanese robata style, so the whole design is unified around a simple image. Text was printed on normal wrapping paper in order to draw attention to the different texture of the material.

韓国料理と炉端が融合したレストランのレセプションパーティーの案内
「韓式炉端いふう」は韓国料理と日本の炉端を融合した新しいスタイルの店のため、全体的に素朴なイメージでまとめた。通常は包装紙として使われる紙をあえて印刷物に使用し、違った素材感で目を引くことを狙った。

DF, S: CHANTO CO.,LTD.   CD, AD: Yukihiko Uchida   D: Masato Nishide

Invitations

Invitation to new product announcement
This is an invitation to a presentation for Rimmel lipstick, which makes lips look fuller after several weeks of application. There was a deliberate decision not to utilize lips or a lipstick motif in the design. Instead, only the event name Rosso Allegria (meaning "red happiness"), a gummy bear (for a soft impression), and the logo are featured.

イタリアのケータリング会社がプロデュースする新作口紅発表イベントの案内
数週間でふっくらした唇になるRimmelの口紅の発表会の招待状。あえて唇や口紅のモチーフは使わず、イベント名Rosso Allegria（赤い幸せ）とクマ型のグミ（柔らかさを表現）とロゴのみを掲載している。

DF, S: Cacao Design   CL: Rimmel / Tribu   CD: Mauro Pastore / Masa Magnoni / Alessandro Floridia
D: Paolo Sala

Invitations

Invitation to an event organized by a caterer in Milan
Tribu is a leading catering service in Milan. This is an invitation to an event produced by Tribu that took place for four days during the MilanoVendeModa fashion fair. It incorporates a genuine clothes hanger and sewing machine stitching.

ミラノのケータリング会社が開催するイベントへの招待状（兼メニュー案内）
Tribuはミラノ屈指のケータリング・サービス。これは、Tribuがプロデュースする4日間のMilanoVendeModaファッション・フェアの招待状で、本物のハンガーとミシン縫い加工を採用している。

DF, S: Cacao Design　CL: Tribu　CD: Mauro Pastore / Masa Magnoni　CD, D: Alessandro Floridia

Invitations

1
Invitations to printing company event for awarded product
These invitations were for an event to publicly present a calendar that had received an award. Actual objects represented in the calendar are enclosed in the invitations. Each package contains a different object, the idea being that several invited guests from the same company will each receive different objects.

印刷会社の受賞イベント招待状（受賞したカレンダーに掲載のオブジェ入）
印刷大賞を受賞したカレンダーのお披露目会の招待状。カレンダーに掲載されたオブジェが入っている。同企業の数人を招待する際、みな中身の違う招待状を受け取ることができるよう1つ1つ違うオブジェが入っている。

DF, S: Cacao Design   CL: Fontegrafica   CD: Mauro Pastore / Masa Magnoni / Alessandro Floridia
D: Paolo Sala

2
Invitation to a "murder mystery" dinner party
Invited guests receive a black box, a CD mailer that has been spray-painted black. It conveys the idea of a murder mystery, with crime scene tape, blood splatters, and fingerprints.

犯人あてゲームを盛り込んだ「殺人ミステリー」ディナーパーティーの招待状
招待客が受け取るのは黒い箱。これはCD郵送用ケースをスプレーで黒く塗ったもので、立入り禁止テープ、血しぶき、指紋などを付けることで殺人ミステリーの雰囲気を演出している。

S: LL Design   CL: Diane Haddock   CD, AD, D: Lisa Leonard-Koger   CW: Kevin kalley

Invitations

Invitation to dinner with Maria Sharapova
The purpose of these invitations is to shatter received expectations so as to make an impression on influential editors. Maria Sharapova is famous for her beauty but she is also a real athlete, and the invitations present both faces in order to convey its message.

マリア・シャラポアとのディナーへの招待状
影響力のあるエディター達の眼鏡に適うような意外性のある招待状を目指した。その美貌で世間を賑わせているシャラポアだが、真のアスリートでもある、というメッセージを伝えるべく、彼女の2つの顔を表現した。

S: ceft and company   CL: New York, NY   CD: Ucef Hanjani   AD: Kimberley Norcott

055

Invitation for a children's clothing collection
Originality was stressed for this invitation, which features eyes made out of chocolates that were specially ordered from a confectioner based on the motif of the brand name, Il Gufo (owl). It was very well-received.

ブランド名 Il Gufo (ふくろう) がモチーフの、子供服コレクションの告知
オリジナリティのあるインビテーションとするため、ブランド名の「Il Gufo=ふくろう」をモチーフとし、菓子店に特注したチョコレートで目を表現。好評を博した。

S: Daniela Vascellari   CL: Il Gufo Spa   CD, AD: Giovanni Frison

Invitations

1

Invitation to an exhibition for a brand of ink
This invitation was sent by international ink maker Huber to printing companies and graphic artists. The aim was to gain recognition for a new color standard to replace Pantone, so the invitation itself included color samples that can be removed.

カラーチップとして使える、世界的なインクブランド Huber の展示会招待状
世界的なインクブランドHuberが、印刷会社、グラフィック・アーティストに送付した招待状。パントーンに代わる新スタンダードとして認められることを目指し、招待状自体を切り取って使える色見本とした。

DF, S: Joseph Rossi srl   CL: Huber spa   D: Graphic First Aid

Invitation to an exhibition of lighting equipment
This invitation is for an international lighting exhibition organized by Ono Luce, an Italian brand of lamps. By using ink that absorbs light and thus can be read in a dark place, they emphasized the concept of "light".

光るインクで「ライト」のコンセプトを強調した、照明器具展覧会の案内
照明器具を扱うイタリアのブランドONO LUCEが開催する国際ライティング・エキシビションの招待状。光を吸収して暗闇でも読むことができるインクを使用し、「ライト」というコンセプトを強調している。

DF, S: Joseph Rossi srl   CL: Ono Luce   D: Graphic First Aid

2

Invitations

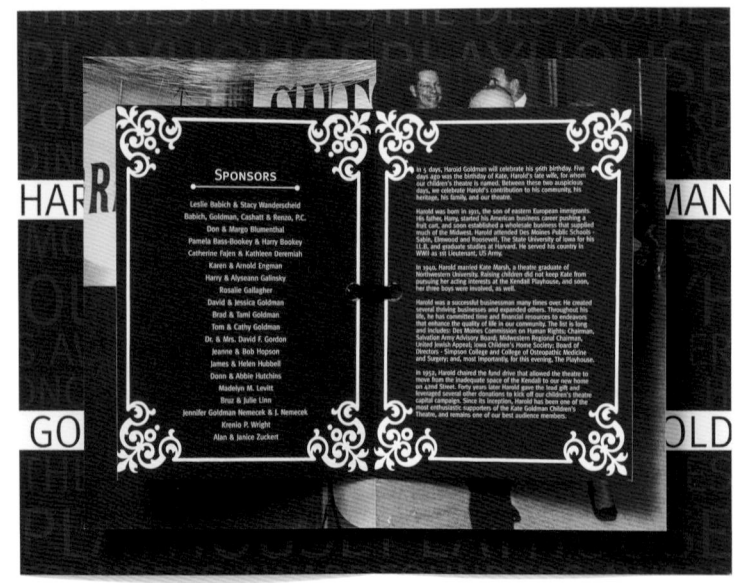

Announcement for an event honoring the Des Moines Theater's Harry Goldman
An invitation to an event honoring Harry Goldman, a prominent Des Moines businessman. The photos in the invitation describe his life. The varying sizes of pages and the ribbon that binds the invitation all make it interesting and impressive.

デモイン劇場の発展に貢献したハリー・ゴールドマンを称えるイベントの案内
デモイン劇場の有名なビジネスマン、ハリー・ゴールドマンの名誉を称えるイベントの招待状。彼の生涯を綴った写真を使用。違う大きさのページとそれをまとめるリボンが面白さとインパクトを与えている。

DF, S: Sayles Graphic Design CL: Des Moines Playhouse CD, AD, D, I: John Sayles
D: Bridget Drendel

Invitations

Announcement for the premier party of "The One", new album by Shinichi Osawa

This direct mail was for a party organized by Zadig & Voltaire, an apparel brand. The direct mail was suggested by a foreign picture book. It was printed on PP-treated material so that when the black-and-white photo is pulled a color photo is revealed.

大沢伸一のニューアルバム「The One」プレミア・パーティー告知

アパレルブランド Zadig & VoltaireによるパーティーのDM。海外で見つけた仕掛け絵本をヒントに制作。PP素材に印刷し、モノクロ写真を引き抜くとカラー写真が現れる仕掛けを施した。

CD, AD, D, S: Nesco　DF: Nigrec Design　CL: Zadig & Voltaire

059

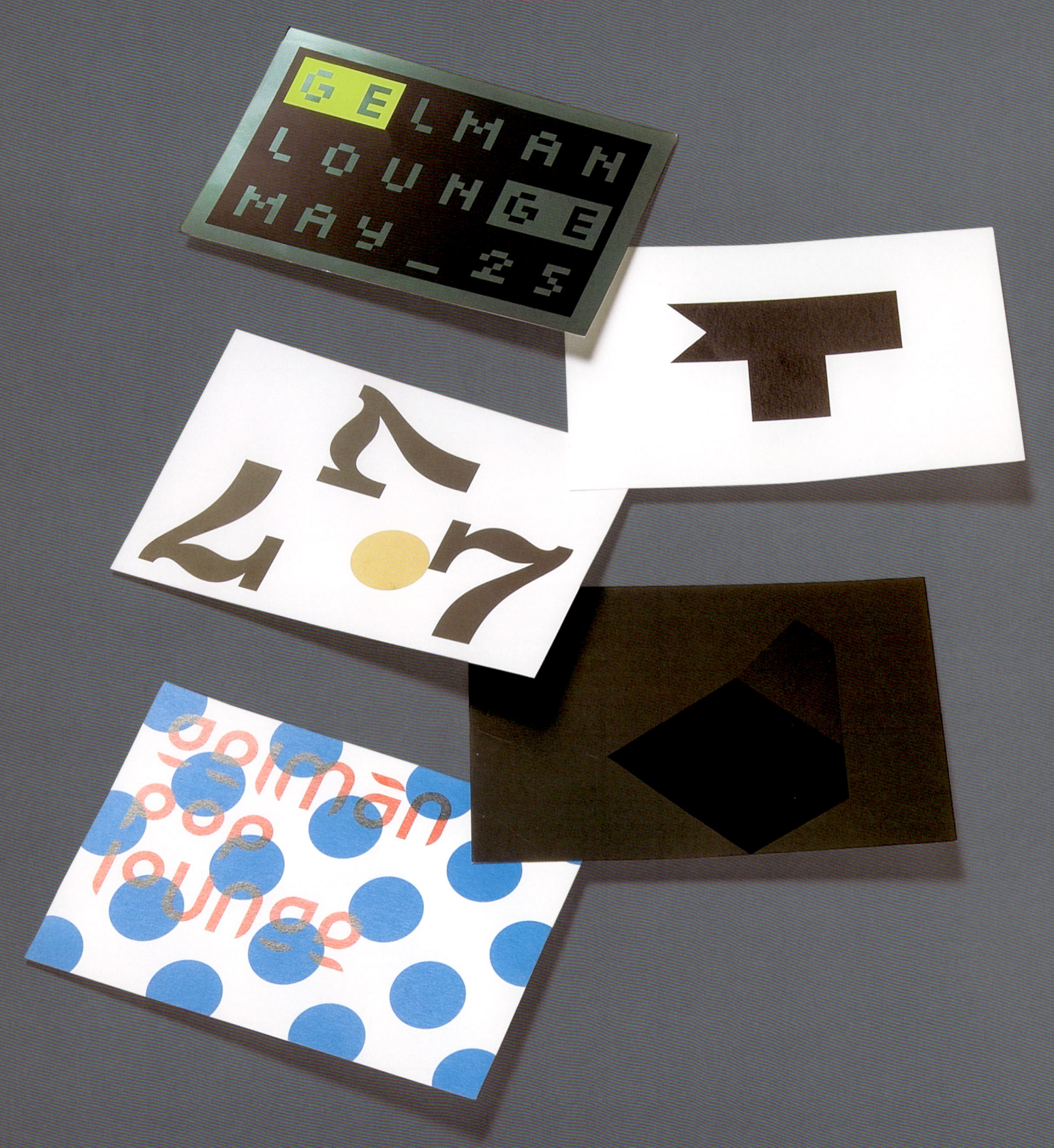

Simple design with a hidden message to raise interest
This series of invitations have a dual function: they can be sent out in envelopes or distributed as flyers, depending on the need. The designs vary but all adhere to a graceful simplicity using special paper, inks, and printing techniques for a consistent effect.

潔いデザインが目を引くパーティー・インビテーション・シリーズ
封筒に入れて送ることができ、必要に応じてフライヤーとしても使えることを考慮した招待状のシリーズ。デザインは違っても同等の効果を生み出せるよう、潔い表現、適切な紙、特殊印刷を選択している。

CD, AD, D, S: Alexander Gelman   DF: Studio Glmn   CL: Nanzuka Underground / Minimal Tokyo / Gelman Lounge

Invitations

Event announcement for PR company based on "hand memo"
The purpose of these invitations was to recall those times when you need to take a memo and the only available medium is your hand, so they instructed guests to not only arrive with invitations in hand but also hand-in-hand. Characters were written on the hand of the creative director, scanned, and then printed on translucent A3-size paper.

手に大事なことをメモする感覚を思い出させる、PR会社のイベント案内
何か大事なことをメモしたいのに自分の手しか書くものがない、という状況を思い出させることを狙った招待状。クリエイティブディレクターの手に文字を書き、それをスキャンしてA3半透明紙に印刷している。招待客が手に招待状を持って、さらに手と手をとり合ってイベントに来てほしいという思いを込めた。

S: Warmrain   CL: Surgery Public Relations   AD: Mark Lawson Bell   D: Warmrain design team

Invitations

Invitation to a DJ event on the theme of Bjork
This is an invitation to a music session inspired by the music of Bjork and featuring various DJs. The envelopers were made from advertising posters for the event and the record-shaped coasters they contained were the invitations that the recipients use to gain admission.

ビョークをテーマにしたDJイベントへのインビテーション
ミュージシャンBjorkをテーマにした、数人のDJによる音楽セッションへの招待状。イベントの宣伝ポスターで作った封筒に、レコード型コースター（インビテーション）が入っている。

DF, S: Raquel Quevedo　CL: Christopher Ovando David　CD, AD, D, I: Raquel Quevedo Lamaza
I: Marta Rossello

062

Invitations

Environmentally friendly invitation that can be reused
A feminine invitation to publicize the liquor Cointreau to women. It includes a shaker, an cell phone strap, and cocktail recipe booklet. A limited number of 200 were distributed to VIPs, but it was so popular that 200 more were produced.

後から使えて環境に優しい、コアントローの女性向けPRイベント招待状
蒸留酒コアントローを女性にPRするためのフェミニンな招待状。シェイカーと携帯ストラップ、カクテルのレシピブックが付いている。VIPのみに200個限定で配られたが人気が高く追加で200個制作した。

DF, S: orlando facioli design　CD, AD, D, I, P, CW: Orlando Facioli　CL: marco 500

063

Invitations

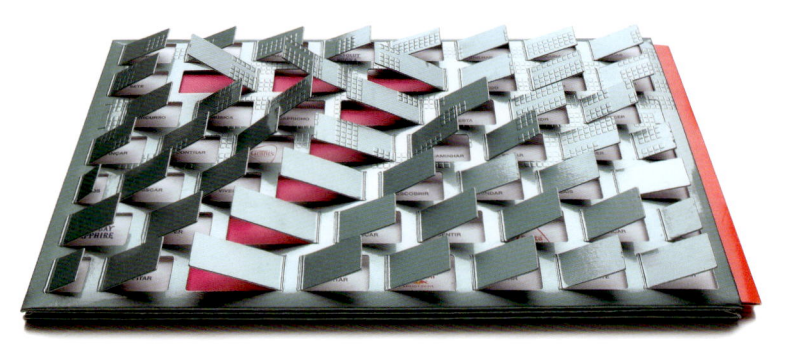

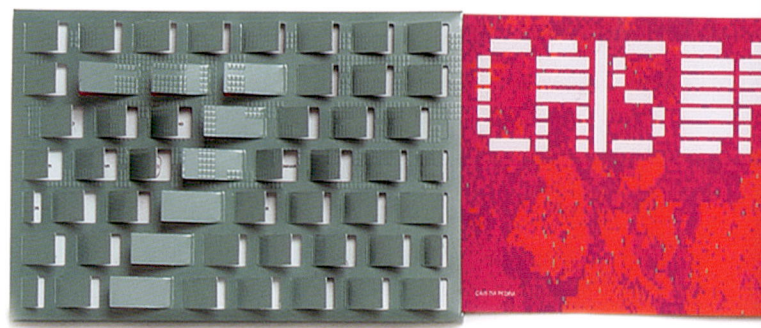

1

Invitation for a 7-year anniversary event
This invitation was for an event to commemorate the seventh anniversary of Lux Fragil, the hippest nightclub in Portugal, located in the port district of Lisbon overlooking the Tejo River. The concept is about color, shape, and mystery.

ナイトクラブ Lux Fragil の7周年記念イベントの招待状
リスボンのウォーターフロントにあり、テージョ川を見渡せる最先端のナイトクラブLux Fragilの7周年を記念するイベントの招待状。コンセプトは色、形、神秘性。

S: RMAC Brand Design CL: Lux Fragil CD: Ricardo Mealha CD, D: Ana Cunha

Direct mail with a new three-dimensional feeling using laminated paper
This direct mail announced the 2008-09 autumn-winter collection for the apparel brand Motel. At a glance, it looks like pressed intaglio (even the printer thought so), but because it uses laminated paper a different nuance is suggested.

合紙により新鮮な立体感を出した、アパレルブランド Motel の告知
アパレルブランドMotelの'08-'09秋冬コレクションの告知DM。一見、型押しのように見えるが（印刷業者も間違える）、合紙を使用しているため、また少し違ったニュアンスが生まれている。

CD, AD, D, S: Nesco DF: Nigrec Design CL: Motel Inc.

2

Invitations

Announcement for the collection of Motel, an apparel brand
This announcement for the 2005 spring-summer collection was sent out to publicists and buyers. It features the image of a 1970's antiwar demonstration taken from a television grab and printed on cardboard. When the cardboard cover is removed, the message is revealed.

段ボールの蓋を開くとメッセージが出てくる、Motel のコレクション案内
PR関係者＆バイヤーに送付した'05春夏コレクションの告知。70年代の反戦運動の段ボールのテロップをイメージしている。段ボールの蓋を開くとメッセージが出てくる仕組み。

CD, AD, D, S: Nesco   DF: Nigrec Design   CL: Motel Inc.

065

Invitations

Announcement of an exhibition for an apparel brand stressing substance

Since this was a joint exhibition for two brands, information for each brand took up one half of the invitation. Laminated paper was used and on the fold of the double doors there are two directions for the sheath, thus providing two ways to open the invitation and making it possible to promote both brands in one mailing.

2方向に開く観音開きで、2ブランドのアピールを可能とした展示会告知

2ブランドの合同展示会だったため、情報を片面ずつに振分けた。合紙を用いており、観音の折り目で刃入れの方向を変え開封方向を2通り用意することで、送付時に両ブランドそれぞれのアピールを可能とした。

CD, AD, D, S: Nesco   DF: Nigrec Design   CL: GOLDWIN

invitations

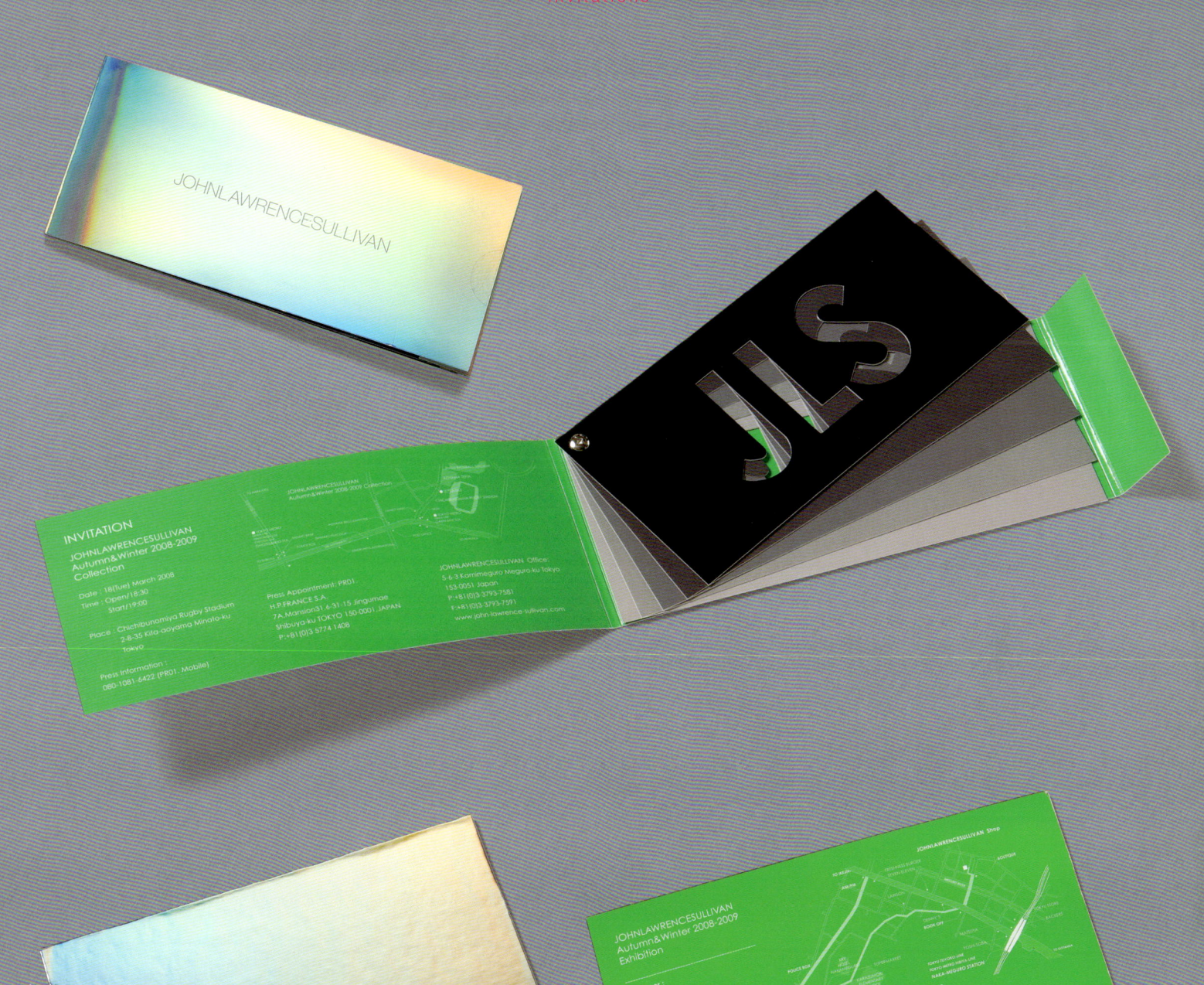

Direct mail that expresses a sharp and graceful brand image
This direct mail announcement was for an exhibition of the 2008-09 autumn-winter collection from JOHNLAWRENCESULLIVAN, an apparel brand. The announcement is elegant and glossy, with a classical serenity that expresses the brand image. Laminated and other specialty papers were used.

シャープさ、優雅さをもつブランドのイメージをDM上で表現
アパレルブランド JOHNLAWRENCESULLIVANの'08−'09秋冬展示会およびコレクションの告知DM。ブランドイメージとして想起されるエレガントな光沢、クラシックな雄々しさなどを表現。合紙および特殊紙を使用。

CD, AD, D, S: Nesco　DF: Nigrec Design　CL: JOHNLAWRENCESULLIVAN

067

Invitations

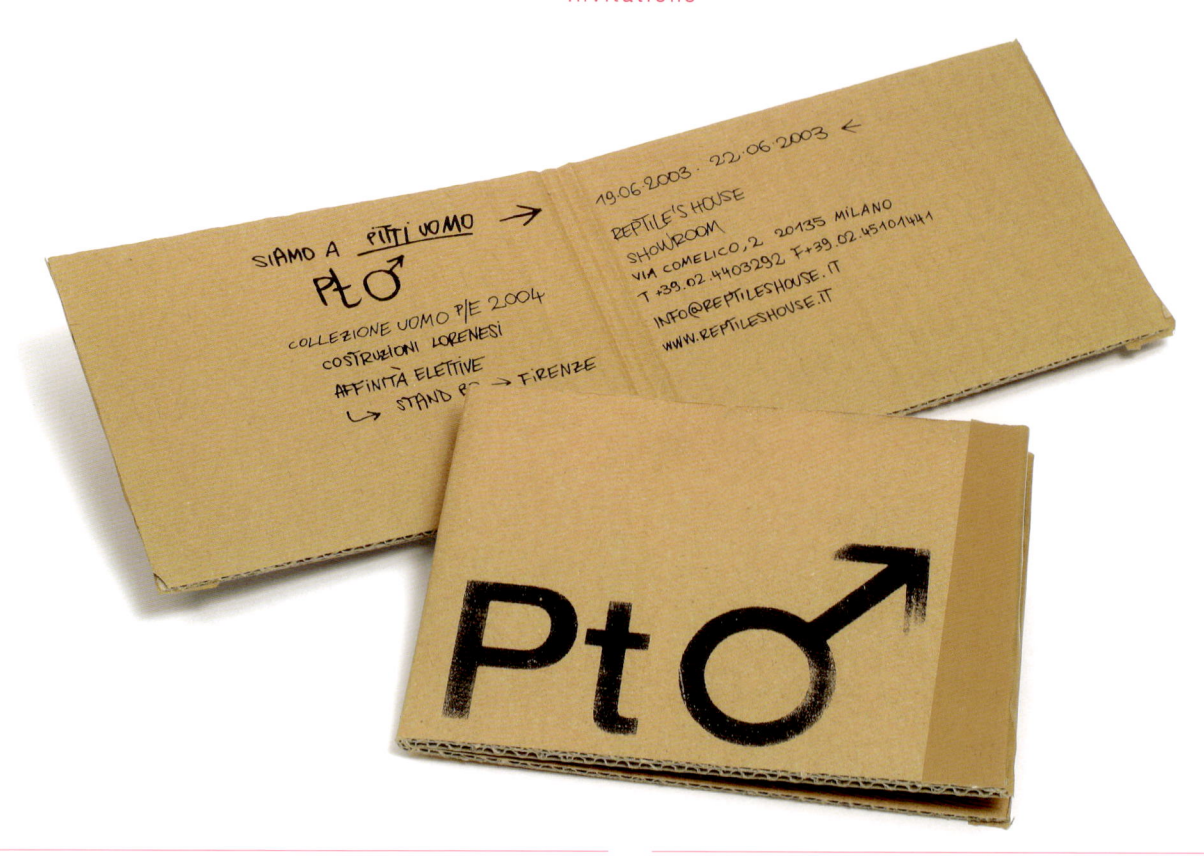

1

Invitation to RH milano fashion fair
RH milano, a brand of bags and belts, produced this invitation for Pitto Uomo, an exhibition in Florence. The corrugated cardboard card features a silkscreen print and is sealed with packing tape.

RH milanoのファッション・フェアのインビテーション
バッグ、ベルトを扱うブランドRHが、フィレンツェで開催される展示会Pitti Uomoのために制作した招待状。シルクスクリーン印刷された段ボールのカードを梱包用テープで留めている。

DF, S: jekyll & hyde   CL: Reptile's House   CD: Marco Molteni / Margherita Monguzzi

2

Announcement of a conference by the investment bank Nordea
This letter of invitation conveyed the Nordic trait of never forgetting and always paying attention to details even when it comes to financial matters. The gift box contains dried leaves with a scent of trees indigenous to Nordic countries.

ドライリーフで北欧らしさを表現した金融グループNordeaの会議案内
金融業界においても細部への配慮を忘れない北欧らしさを伝える招待状。ギフトボックスには北欧の木々のエッセンスで香りづけされたドライリーフが入っている。

S: room corporation   CL: nordea   CD: Paolo Prossen

Invitations

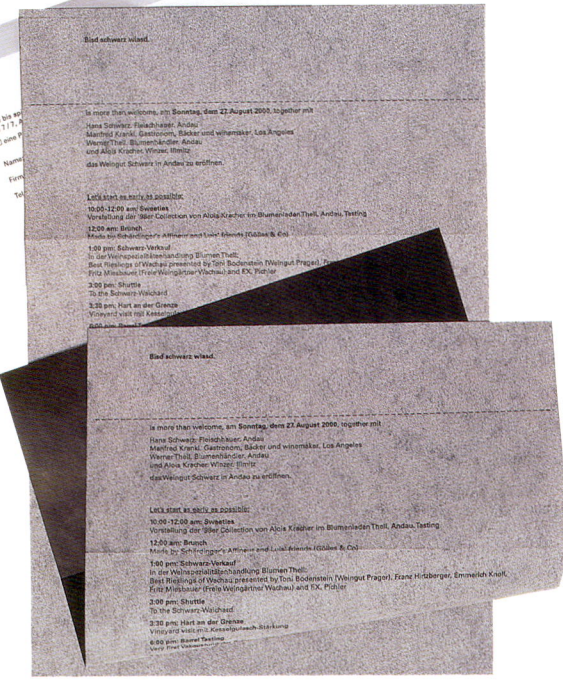

Invitation to a new product presentation event
This invitation was for an event promoting a new wine called "Black" from Schwarz. The vintner's main business is that of a butcher, so the text was printed on paper used for wrapping sausage. The paper is backed with carbon so that when you touch it your fingers are stained with black ink.

触ると手が黒くなる、ワインメーカーの新商品「ブラック」の発表会招待状
Schwarzの新しいワイン「ブラック」の発表イベントの招待状。ワイン栽培者の本業が肉屋であることから、テキストはソーセージの包装紙に印刷。裏側はカーボンなので、触ると黒インクが手に付いてしまう。

DF, S: alessandridesign   CL: HANS SCHWARZ, ALOIS KRACHER, MANFRED KRANKL
CD, AD: Cordula Alessandri   CW: Dorli Muhr

069

Invitations

Invitation to the final party for members salon CELUX
In order to convey the Cabaret party theme, the event was expressed using heart bubble wrap and metallic paper. Inside the wrapping is a special-order Vuitton bracelet and a CD. It conveyed CELUX's playful attitude with a luxurious and casual intention.

会員制サロン CELUX のファイナル・パーティーの招待状
パーティーのテーマ「キャバレー」に合わせ、ハートのプチプチ×メタリック紙でイベントのノリを表現。中にはヴィトン特注のブレスレットやCD等を同封。豪華さと軽さの対比もCELUXの遊び心を表している。

DF, S: CAP Inc.　CL: CELUX COMPANY LVJ GROUP K.K.　AD: Yasushi Fujimoto　D: Hiromi Fujita

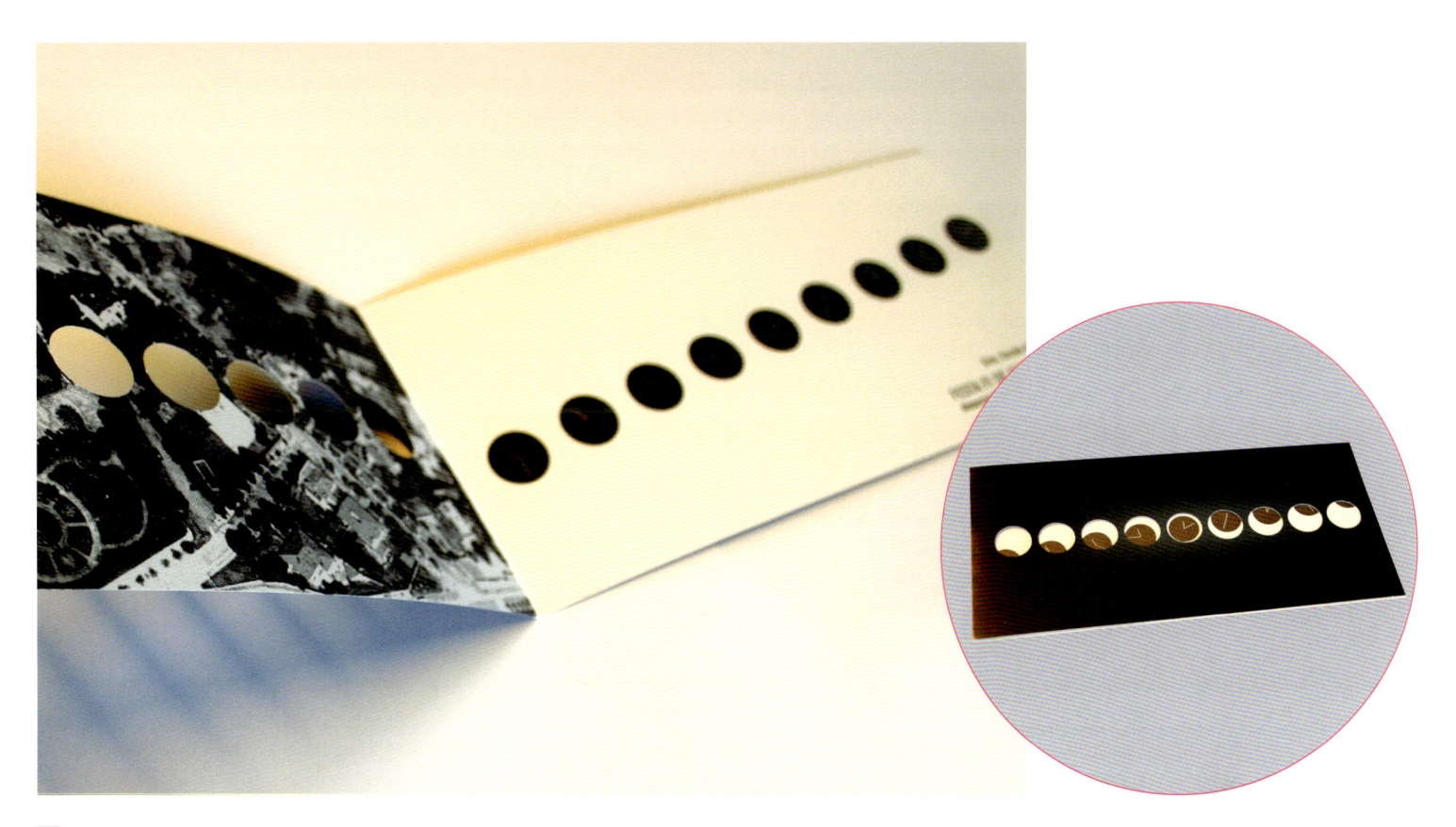

Invitations

1
Invitation to a graduation party
Invitation to the 2006 graduation party for the art school Eina. The theme was a lunar eclipse. The silhouettes seen through the die-cut circles double as clocks, indicating the time period of the party.

月食をテーマにしたアートスクールの卒業パーティーへの案内状
アートスクールEINAの2006年の卒業パーティーのインビテーション。テーマは「月食」。型抜きした穴から見える影の部分は時計にもなっていて、パーティーの開催時間を示している。

CL, S: Eina,Escola De Disseny i Art   D: Lluc Massaguer Busqueta

2
Invitation to an art exhibition of couples' costumes entitled "○ Exhibition"
Because it is related to an installation featuring couples' costumes, the concept of the design is based on a donut shape. People found this direct mail very charming, and it helped increase the number of visitors to the event. Many guests kept the invitation as a decorative memento.

ドーナツ型がとてもチャーミングな、アート展の招待状
カップルのコスチュームをつなげてみせていくコンセプトを、ドーナツ型にデザインすることで表現した。このDMがチャーミングと評判で、来場者を増やすことにひと役買った。部屋の飾りにしている人も多い。

CD, AD, I, S: Hisashi Narita   D: Shintaro Tagashira

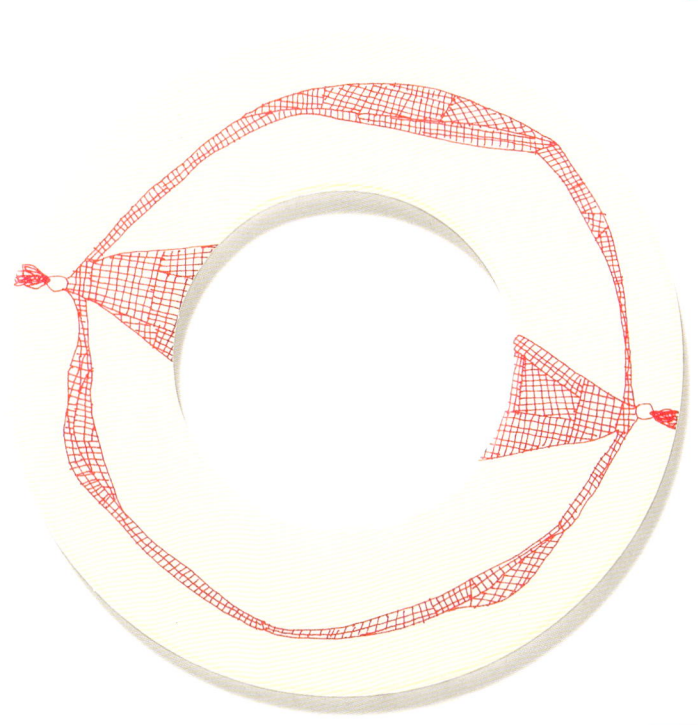

071

Invitations

1
Announcement of a fashion fair for shoemaker Bravo
An invitation to an exhibition for the Bravo shoe brand. The design makes for an interesting card in terms of appearance and texture through a combination of materials and the use of a powerful illustration.

シューズ・ブランドBravoのファッション・フェアのお知らせ
シューズ・ブランドBravoの展示会の招待状。さまざまな違う素材の組み合わせや、パワフルなイラストレーションを採用することにより、見た目も手触りも面白いカードに仕上がった。

DF, S: Happycentro+Sintetik　CL: Bravo　CD, AD, D, I: Federico Galvani

Invitation to a presentation of new U'Luvka Vodka co-organized by a lingerie brand
This invitation is for a party co-organized by lingerie brand Coco De Mer. The purpose is to attract the attention of VIPs. When the handknit ribbon is untied, the envelope, which is black leaf on black paper, opens to reveal an invitation and an RSVP card.

ランジェリーブランドと共催したウルヴカウォッカの新商品発表の招待状
ランジェリーブランドCoco De Merとの共催によるパーティーの招待状。VIPの目にも留まるものを目指した。黒い紙に黒の箔押しをした封筒の手編みのリボンを解くと、招待状と返信用カードが入っている。

DF, S: Aloof Design　CL: The Brand Distillery　CD: Sam Aloof　D: Andrew Scrase

Invitations

Direct mail that functions as something other than an announcement

This direct mail was for the 2007-08 autumn-winter collection as well as the 2008 spring-summer collection of Zadiq & Voltaire. The design was based on a sightseeing map from a foreign country. When the envelope is opened the catalogue unfolds like an accordion. On the back is a large poster.

裏面がポスターになった、アパレルブランドのコレクションのお知らせ

Zadig & Voltaireの'07-'08秋冬および'08春夏コレクションのDM。海外で見つけた観光マップを参考に制作。開封すると蛇腹折りのカタログが展開され、裏面は大判のポスターになっている。

CD, AD, D, S: Nesco   DF: Nigrec Design   CL: Zadig & Voltaire

073

Invitations

1
Tear-off direct mail with a memo pad motif
This direct mail announcement was for the summer exhibition of the apparel brand Motel. The design takes advantage of the structure of a memo pad and the feeling of tearing off a sheet. The information is hidden inside. UV pressure sensitive adhesive is not used. Instead the three sides of the memo pad are glued together.

メモパッドのように剥がす構造を採用したアパレルブランドの告知DM
アパレルブランドMotelのサマーエキシビションの告知DM。メモパッドを剥がす感触とその構造を参考にしている。情報は内部に秘匿されているが、UV圧着ではなく3辺をメモパッド状に糊付けしている。

CD, AD, D, S: Nesco   DF: Nigrec Design   CL: Motel Inc.

Select shop invitation that's fun to open
This invitation was for a press exhibition of nano・universe. In order to read the invitation the recipient has to tear the package, as if opening a pack of candy or cosmetics, the idea being that the recipient is "removing sealed information." The texture and the feeling of anticipation when opening the package are expressed on the flat direct mail.

バリバリと開ける感触が面白い、セレクトショップのインビテーション
nano・universeのプレスエキシビションの招待状。「閉じ込められた情報を取り出す」という考え方で、お菓子や化粧品のパッケージのように剥がして読ませる仕組み。開封時の感触と期待感をDM上で平面化し再現している。

S: Nesco   DF: Nigrec Design   CD, AD, D: Satoko Matsui   CL: nano・universe

2

074

Invitations

1
Collection announcement with message readable through envelope window
This invitation is for an exhibition of the spring-summer collection of Men's Bigi, an apparel brand. A window envelope was used, and by changing the usual position of the window an old idea was made new.

封筒窓から招待状のメッセージが読める、アパレルブランドのコレクション案内
アパレルブランドMEN'S BIGIの春夏コレクション展示会のインビテーション。採用しているのは窓開き封筒の技術だが、位置を変えることで新鮮なデザインに。

S: antenna graphic base   CL: MEN'S BIGI Co.,Ltd.   AD, D: Akira Sumi

2
Invitation for an exhibition of Cinzia Maini Jewellery
A velvet card was wrapped in two pieces of paper decorated in an old English style. The design of the invitation stressed the texture, which is appropriate for an exhibition of a luxury jewelry designer.

イタリアの宝飾ブランド Cinzia Maini のリュクスな展示会案内
ベルベットのようなカードを、2枚の紙で包み、オールド・イングランドを意識したデコレーションをあしらった。ジュエリーデザイナーのラグジュアリな展示会にふさわしい素材感を重視したインビテーションとした。

DF, S: Joseph Rossi srl   CL: Cinzia Maini   D: Graphic First Aid

Invitations

1

Invitation to a presentation of the new MINI model
The invitations were sent to VIPs in the movie industry. The concept is "top secret". The booklet contains a script for a non-existent movie and the text describes the content of the event.

トップシークレットの文字が興味をそそる MINI の新車発表会の招待状
映画業界のVIPに送られた招待状。コンセプトは「トップシークレット」。中に入っている冊子は、偽ものの映画の台本で、テキストは、イベントの内容に対応している。

DF, S: Oktober Kommunikationsdesign GmbH   CL: BMW-Group   CD: Silke Lohmann
AD, D: Nadine Fliegen   CW: Christian Kreienkamp

Exhibition announcement for RH Milano using olive and harvest bag motif
This invitation from RH milano suggests an olive grove. The invitation was produced for the trade show White, which takes place in Milan. The source of the inspiration for the new collection was the bags used for harvesting olives. The holes represent olives.

オリーブの実と収穫用鞄をモチーフにした RH Milano の展示会案内
ミラノで開かれるトレードショーWhiteのために制作した招待状。新作コレクションのインスピレーションの源は、かつてオリーブの収穫に使われていた鞄。たくさんの穴によりオリーブの実を表現した。

DF, S: jekyll & hyde   CL: RH milano   CD: Marco Molteni / Margherita Monguzzi   P: Orazio Truglio

2

Invitations

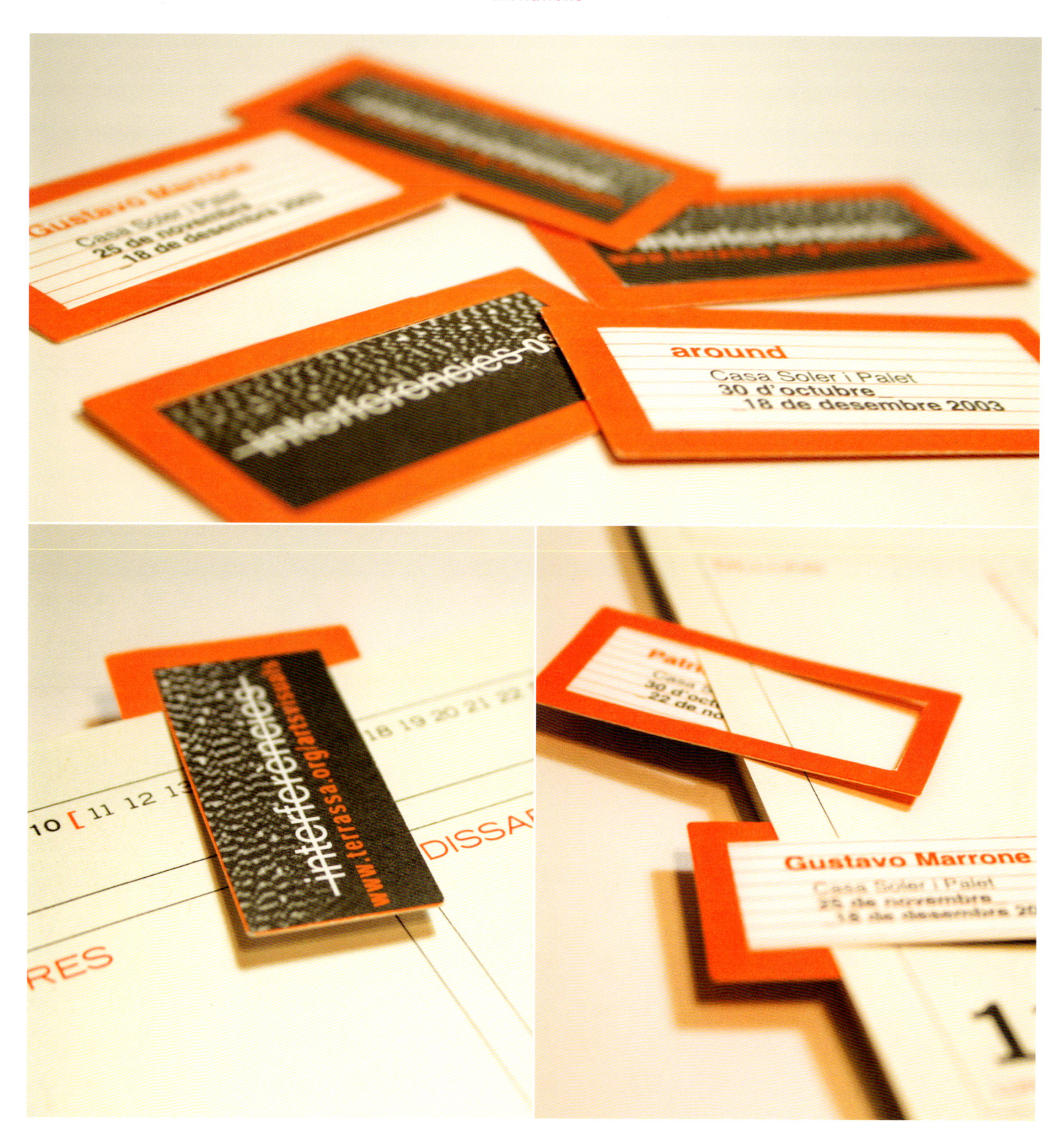

Culture event invitation that uses a new type of stationery
This invitation is for a culture event, including a contemporary art exhibition, organized by the town council of Terrassa in Barcelona. The card that contains the event information is in the form of a clip that can be used with a personal diary.

ステーショナリー感覚が新しい、カルチャー・イベントの招待状
バルセロナのテラッサという街の市議会が主催する、現代アートの展覧会をはじめとする文化イベントへのインビテーション。イベント情報が掲載されたカードはクリップの形になっており、手帳などに付けられる。

D, S: Lluc Massaguer Busqueta　CL: Ajuntament De Terrassa

077

Invitations

Announcement expressing the concept of visualization using cylinder image
A major printing company was rebranded and changed its logo in line with the concept of "image reflection." This is an invitation to the related CI presentation event, which was held at the Terrazza Martini in Milan.

円筒に図像を映像化（イメージ・リフレクション）してコンセプトを表現した、印刷会社のCI発表会の案内
大手印刷会社が「イメージ・リフレクション（イメージの反映）」をメイン・コンセプトとしてリブランドし、イメージとロゴを一新。これは、ミラノのTerrazza Martiniで開催したCI発表イベントの招待状。

DF, S: Cacao Design   CL: Fontegrafica   CD: Mauro Pastore / Masa Magnoni / Alessandro Floridia
D, I: Paolo Sala

Invitations

Invitation to a topping off ceremony from a real estate company
This invitation is to a topping off ceremony for New Street Square, which was built in the center of London. The designer emphasized a sense of fun by enclosing party favors. The design was playful and pleased both the client and the client's guests.

パーティーグッズで楽しさを演出する、不動産会社による落成式への招待状
ロンドンの中心に建設されたニューストリート・スクエアの落成を祝うセレモニーへの招待状。息を吹き入れると伸びるおもちゃでパーティーの楽しさを演出。遊び心のあるデザインは依頼主にも招待客にも喜ばれた。

S: Studio 6.3 and Zulver & Co   CL: Land Securities   CD: Micheal Smith   D: Ben Cox / Keith Anderson
DF: Zulver & Co

079

Invitations

Announcement of new office opening featuring a hidden key
People tend to hide door keys under their door mats so that friends can use them when they are not at home. This invitation contained a map, a key, and a mini-mat with welcome printed on it.

ドアマットの下に鍵が隠れた、デザイン会社の新事務所オープニング案内
ドアマットは留守中に友達に鍵を渡したいときに鍵を隠す場所であることから、インビテーションにはマップと鍵と、「Welcome」と書かれたミニマットが入っている。

CL, DF, S: MATITE GIOVANOTTE   CD, AD, I: Alberto Cassani   AD: Giovanni Pizzigati   D: Luca Raggi
CW: Antonella Bandou

080

Invitations

1

Matchbook-shaped graduation party invitation that uses black humor
Invitation to the 2005 graduation party for the art school Eina. That year there was a fire at the school so they came up with the bold idea of using a matchbook as a motif.

火事があった年の卒業パーティー招待状は、ブラックユーモア溢れるマッチ型
アートスクールEINAの2005年の卒業パーティーのインビテーション。この年、学校に火事があったことから、マッチをモチーフにするという大胆な発想。

CL, S: Eina,Escola De Disseny i Art   D: Lluc Massaguer Busqueta

2

Invitation to the opening of the select shop nano·universe
This box-shaped invitation contains a novelty and was sent to publicists, stylists, and others. The main color is gold and novelty pin badges are enclosed.

セレクトショップ nano·universe のオープニング・インビテーション
PR関係者、スタイリスト、その他関係者をターゲットにした、ノベルティーが入るボックス型の招待状。金色を主体とし、ノベルティーのピンバッチが入っている。

CD, AD, D, S: Nesco   DF: Nigrec Design   CL: nano·universe

Invitations

WIR
SCHWIMMEN
NICHT
IM GELD …

Direct mail for a children's welfare NPO
An announcement to solicit donations for an NPO. Contributors who made donations of at least one thousand euros were given "SmileStone Awards," and the trophy attached to the card is half the size of the real trophy. There are four more types of trophies, the idea being that contributors may want to collect all five trophies.

寄付者に贈られるトロフィーをかたどった児童福祉NPOの寄付募集の案内
団体への寄付募集の案内。千ユーロ以上の寄付者にはスマイル・ストーン賞が贈られるが、カードに付いているのは実際のトロフィの1/2サイズ。他にも4種のトロフィがあり、コレクションする寄付者も出てきた。

S: Kurt Dornig Graphikdesign & Illustration   CL: Netz fur Kinder   D: Kurt Dornig

Invitations

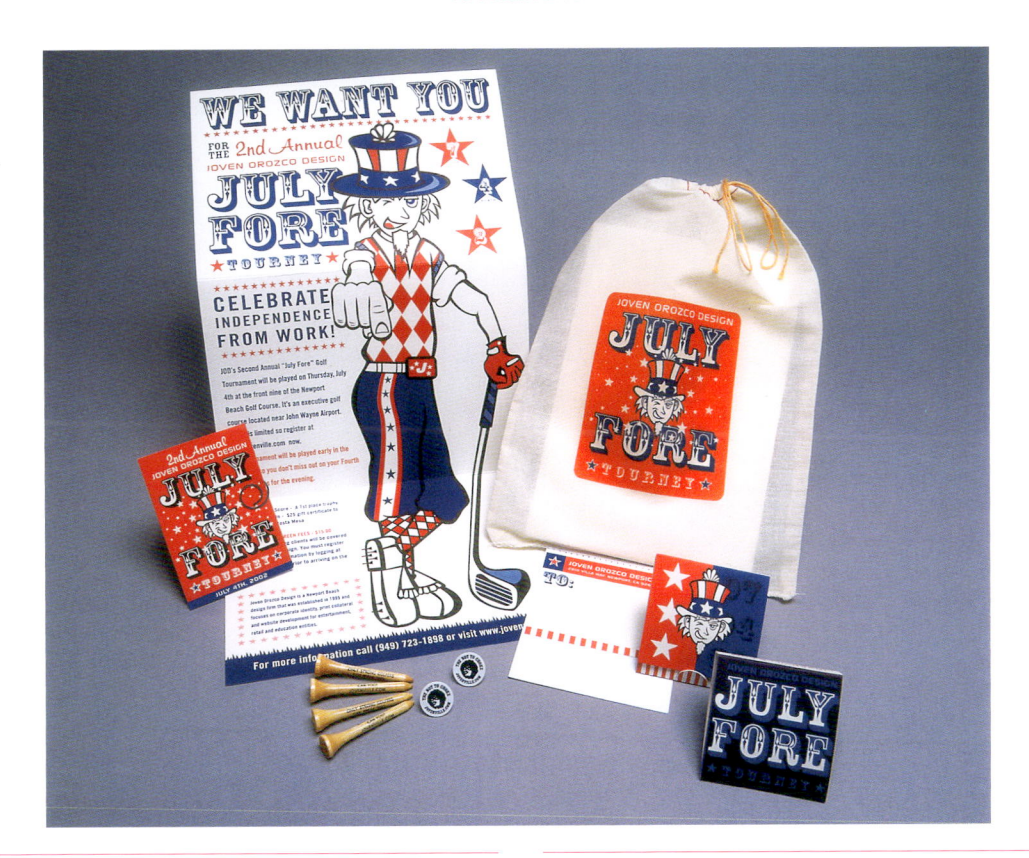

1

Invitation to a golf tournament organized by a design company
Invitation to an annual golf tournament held by a design company. The purpose of the invitation is to remind recipients of the design company's existence. Because the tournament date is Independence Day, the concept is a more contemporary-style Uncle Sam saying that "we want you" to attend.

デザイン会社主催の毎年恒例ゴルフ・イベントへの招待状
デザイン会社主催で毎年開催しているゴルフ・トーナメントへの招待状。自社の存在を思い出してもらうことも狙い。開催日（独立記念日）にちなんで、コンセプトは「皆の参加を待つ、今風のアンクル・サム」。

CL, DF, S: Joven Orozco Design　CD: Joven Orozco　AD, D: Kenneth Lim　D, I: John Garcia

Invitation to a golf tournament in the shape of a cracker
This invitation was sent out to companies that the sender already does business with, as well as companies the sender wants to do business with. They used a unique firecracker design to convey the idea that the event will be very special. Inside the cracker is a matchbook with information about the event, as well as golf-related items. The year the company used this particular invitation more companies attended the event than ever before.

デザイン会社主催ゴルフ・トーナメントのクラッカー型インビテーション
取引先・顧客候補に送付した招待状。ユニークなクラッカー型を採用し、特別なイベントであると期待させるデザインに。中には情報の書かれたマッチ、ゴルフグッズが入っている。この年は多くの参加者が集まった。

CL, DF, S: Joven Orozco Design　CD, D, I: Joven Orozco　AD, D, I, P: Kenneth Lim

2

083

Invitations

Invitation to celebrate the 20th anniversary of a design studio
Clients, suppliers, friends, and family were invited to the celebration. In line with the coaster-invitations, pint glasses printed with the company's logo, which had been redesigned earlier that year, were given to guests as they left the party.

デザインスタジオの20周年記念パーティーの招待状
クライアント、サプライヤー、友人や家族を招いてパーティーを開催。コースター型インビテーションに合わせて、パーティーの帰り際には、この年リニューアルした同社のロゴをあしらったパイント・グラスを贈った。

CL, DF, S: Real Art Design Group,Inc.   CD: Chris Wire   AD: Jeremy Loyd   D: Crystal Dennis

Invitations

Invitation for an event at a Des Moines art center
An invitation to an annual sale. The main motif was "Under the Big Top," a story about a circus, which is the main theme. Guests receive posters designed around this theme as a memento.

サーカスをテーマにしたデモイン・アートセンターのイベント招待状
毎年行われるセールの招待状。メイン・テーマであるサーカスにちなんだ物語『Under the Big Top』がモチーフとなっている。ゲストには記念品として同じテーマでデザインされたポスターが配られた。

DF, S: Sayles Graphic Design　CL: Des Moines Art Center　CD, AD, D, I: John Sayles　D: Bridget Drendel

085

Invitations

Invitations for celebrating induction into Texas Rodeo Cowboy Hall of Fame

Invitations to a party to celebrate the induction of the client's father into a hall of fame. A nostalgic mood is created with a black-and-white photo from the father's childhood that has been colored using Photoshop; the paper is Parchtone; and the invitations are rolled up, tied with leather lacing, and placed in a kraft paper mailing tube.

テキサス・ロデオ・カウボーイズ殿堂入り祝賀会の招待状

依頼主の父親の殿堂入りを祝う会の招待状。父親の少年時代の白黒写真をPhotoshopで彩色、紙はParchtone、丸めた招待状に結ぶ革ひも、クラフト紙の郵送用チューブなどで昔っぽい雰囲気を演出した。

S: LL Design　CL: The Pressley family　CD, AD: Lisa Leonard-Koger

Invitation to a fundraising event for a children's welfare facility

This invitation was for an annual dance and fundraising event at Wildwood Hills Ranch, a non-profit organization that helps disadvantaged children. The illustration and typography recreate the mood of a Western.

西部劇の雰囲気を演出した児童福祉施設の募金イベントの招待状

問題を抱えた子どもを支援する非営利団体ワイルドウッド・ヒルズ・ランチで毎年開かれるダンスパーティーおよび募金イベントへのインビテーション。イラストとタイポグラフィは西部劇の雰囲気を演出している。

DF, S: Sayles Graphic Design　CL: Wildwood Hills Ranch　CD, AD, D, I: John Sayles　D: Bridget Drendel

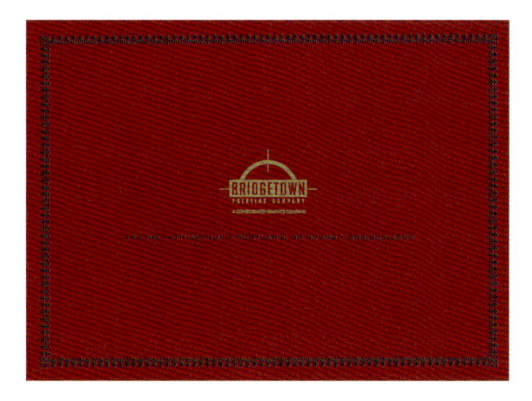

Invitations

1
Invitations to office relocation party
Invitations to a party to show off a company's new offices. The theme is a 1920s carnival. The name of the guest is printed on a special place in the invitation. The purpose of the design is to be eye-catching.

20年代カーニバルをテーマにした、印刷会社の事務所移転パーティー招待状
新しい事業所のお披露目パーティーのための招待状。テーマは1920年代のカーニバル。招待客の名前が入れられるようになっている。受け取った人の興味を引くデザインを目指した。

DF, S: Dotzero Design   CL: Bridgetown Printing   D: Karen Wippich / Jon Wippich
CW: Courtenay Hameister

2
Mysterious invitations using a traditional fortune-teller motif
These invitations were for a presentation of the Maida clothing collection in Naples. It's based on the Neopolitan tradition of Smorfia, fortune-telling cards based on dreams. The numerals stand for the dates of the events while also corresponding to good luck numbers.

伝統的な占いをモチーフにした、アパレルブランドの神秘的なイベント案内
ナポリで行われたMaidaコレクションの発表会への招待状。ナポリの伝統的な夢占い「スモルフィア」をモデルにしている。数字はイベントの日程を表していると同時に、縁起のいい言葉と関連している。

DF, S: Joseph Rossi srl   CL: RGR   D: Graphic First Aid

087

Invitations

Invitation to a Christmas sale at an interior furnishings store
The client promoted a campaign in which customers who attended the
special Christmas sale held by Cariolato would receive hot chocolate.
The embossed invitation cards were made to look like chocolate bars.

エンボスで板チョコを表した、インテリア・ショップのクリスマスセール告知
Cariolato各店舗にて、クリスマス特別セールに訪れたお客さんに、ホットチョコレートを提供するキャンペーンを
開催。エンボス加工が施されたインビテーションカードで、板チョコを表現している。

DF, S: Joseph Rossi srl   CL: Cariolato   D: Graphic First Aid

088

Invitations

1

Invitation to a furniture exhibition
This invitation card was for an exhibition of Baxter, a brand of furniture, that was organized by Cariolato, an interior furnishings store. When the card is folded it shows a sofa for two persons, but when it is opened the sofa seats five, thus promoting the large, high quality sofas that are Baxter's specialty.

カードを開くと特徴的な大型ソファが出てくる家具展示会のお知らせ
インテリアショップCariolatoが開催した家具ブランドBaxterの展示会への招待状。開くと2人掛けから5人掛けソファになるカードが、Baxterの特徴である大型の高級ソファーをアピールしている。

DF, S: Joseph Rossi srl   CL: Cariolato   D: Graphic First Aid

Invitation to a collection held at a race track
This is an invitation to a collection that took place at the San Siro race track in Milan. When the recipient pulls the card, the horse in the square window at the bottom of the card seems to run and writing appears in the rectangular windows.

引き出すと小窓の中の馬が走る、アパレルブランドのコレクション案内
ミラノのSan Siro競馬場で行われるコレクションへのインビテーション。カードを引っ張ると、下部にある正方形の窓に見え隠れする馬が走っているように見え、長方形の窓には文字が現れる。

DF, S: Joseph Rossi srl   CL: SINV   D: Graphic First Aid

2

Invitations

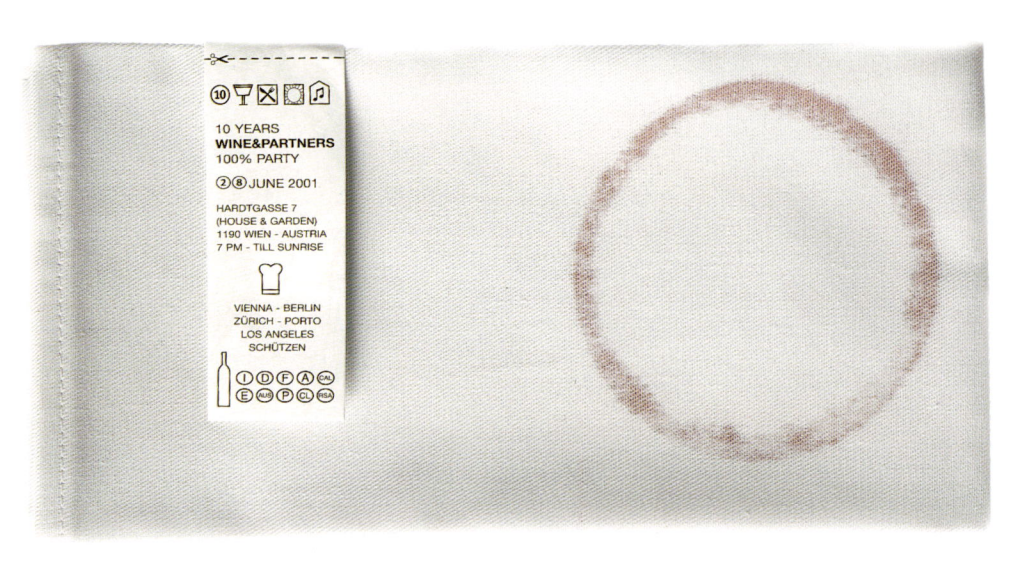

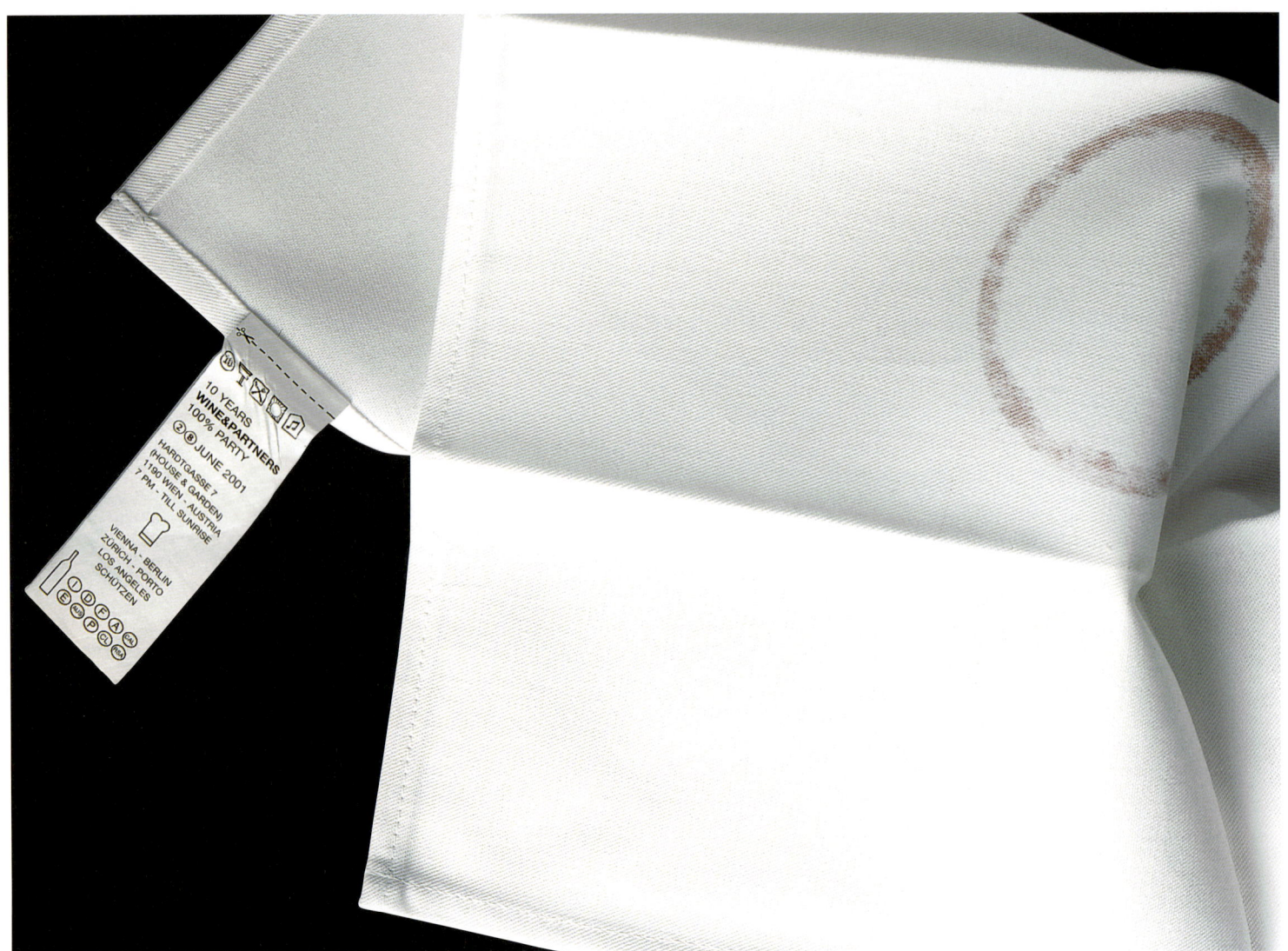

Invitation to a tenth anniversary party
This invitation to a party to commemorate the tenth anniversary of Wine and Partners featured a real napkin with a wineglass stain. The information about the event is printed on the tag.

ワインの染みがユニークな、ワインメーカー10周年記念パーティー案内
ワイン＆パートナーズの10周年記念パーティーの招待客に送られたのは、本物のワイングラスの染みがついたナプキン。イベントに関する情報は、タグに記載されている。

DF, S: alessandridesign   CL: WINE & PARTNERS   CD: Cordula Alessandri   AD: Caroline Bruckner
CW: Cosima Reif   I: Bettina Baeck

Invitations

Direct mail for opening of BC SALON SHIBUYA
This is an announcement for the opening of a building complex for Bay Cruise (a women's fashion building including Journal Standard, Spick and Span, and an isometrics studio). When the announcement is opened the lettering springs up.

ブランド複合ビルBC SALON SHIBUYAのオープニング案内
ベイクルーズのブランド複合ビル（JOURNAL STANDARD、Spick and Span、加圧トレーニングスタジオなど女性のためのファッション・ビル）のオープン告知。開くと文字が飛び出す仕組み。

CL, S: BAYCREW'S Co.,Ltd.   CD, AD, D, DF: Mo-Green Co.,Ltd.   I: Yuko Yamamoto

1

2

Invitation to an exhibition of a Korean brand of paper
An accordion form was utilized so that the invitation could be displayed on a shelf as well as to unify the image in relation to the exhibition, Little Tree. The paper used was Tanto Select. The invitation had a hand in increasing the number of visitors to the exhibition.

じゃばら型を採用した、韓国の紙ブランドの「飾れる」展示会招待状
棚にも飾られるような形状（じゃばら）を採用し、展示会「Little tree」に関連したイメージでまとめた。用紙はタントセレクトを使用。会場への動員数増加にひと買貢った。

DF, S: ONE STROKE Co.,Ltd.   CL: DOOSUNG PAPER   AD: Katsumi Komagata
D, I: Jeong-Won Seo

091

Invitations

1

Invitation to a healing salon (Tsuki no Kakera)
This direct mail publicizes the salon to clients (patients). The outside of the case features a moon, a rabbit, and a heart (cut out) expressed symbolically, When it is opened, there is an origami figure of a rabbit, which the clients have found interesting.

月、うさぎ、心をモチーフにした、ヒーリングサロン「月のかけら」の案内
クライアント(患者)にサロンをPRするためのDM。ケースには、月、うさぎ、心(型抜き)がシンボリックに表現されている。開くとうさぎの折り紙が入っている。クライアントにも喜ばれた。

DF, S: Design Unit RE・Beans　CL: Tsuki no Kakera　CD: Gessin Amano　AD, D: Norio Oka
CW: Ryoko

Announcement for an exhibition based on "seven-color bird" motif
This announcement was for an exhibition of the 2008 spring-summer n°11 Line for pure and attractive women. It includes seven embossed birds in line with the exhibition theme of "L'oiseau aux sept couleurs" (birds of seven colors). The use of colors and illustrations is meant to evoke a fantasy mood.

ブランドn°11ラインの展示会テーマ「七色の鳥」をモチーフにした案内状
純粋で可憐な女性のためのn°11ラインの2008年春夏展示会の案内。「L'oiseau aux sept couleurs(七色の鳥)」というテーマに合わせた7羽のエンボスの鳥がポイント。色使いやイラストが幻想的。

S: SHIMAMURA TOKYO CORPORATION　Director: Kimiko Shimamura

2

Invitations

1

Invitation for an autumn-winter exhibition using warm colors and images
Based on the exhibition theme "The Wispy Memories," this wintry card features graded tones from orange to black to convey warmth and tenderness, thus conjuring up a unique fairy tale world.

アパレルラインn°11の秋冬展示会の招待状は、暖色系で温かなイメージ
展示会のテーマ「the wispy memories」にちなんで、温かで優しいコンセプトを伝えるため、オレンジから黒へのグラデーションを使い、冬らしいカードに。おとぎ話のような独特の世界観が生まれている。

S: SHIMAMURA TOKYO CORPORATION   Director: Kimiko Shimamura

Announcement for autumn-winter exhibition conveying a gentle fantasy atmosphere
The image of a three-dimensional castle and snow dancing in a star-filled sky expresses the theme of the 05-06 autumn-winter, which was "Glorious snow in wonderland." Many recipients said the announcement made it easy to imagine what the clothing looked like.

n°11のファンタジックで優しい雰囲気を伝える秋冬展示会のお知らせ
立体的なお城と夜空に舞う雪をイメージさせる星空が、05-06秋冬展示会のテーマである「glorious snow in wonderland」のコンセプトをうまく表現している。ウエアを想像しやすいという声が多かった。

S: SHIMAMURA TOKYO CORPORATION   Director: Kimiko Shimamura

2

093

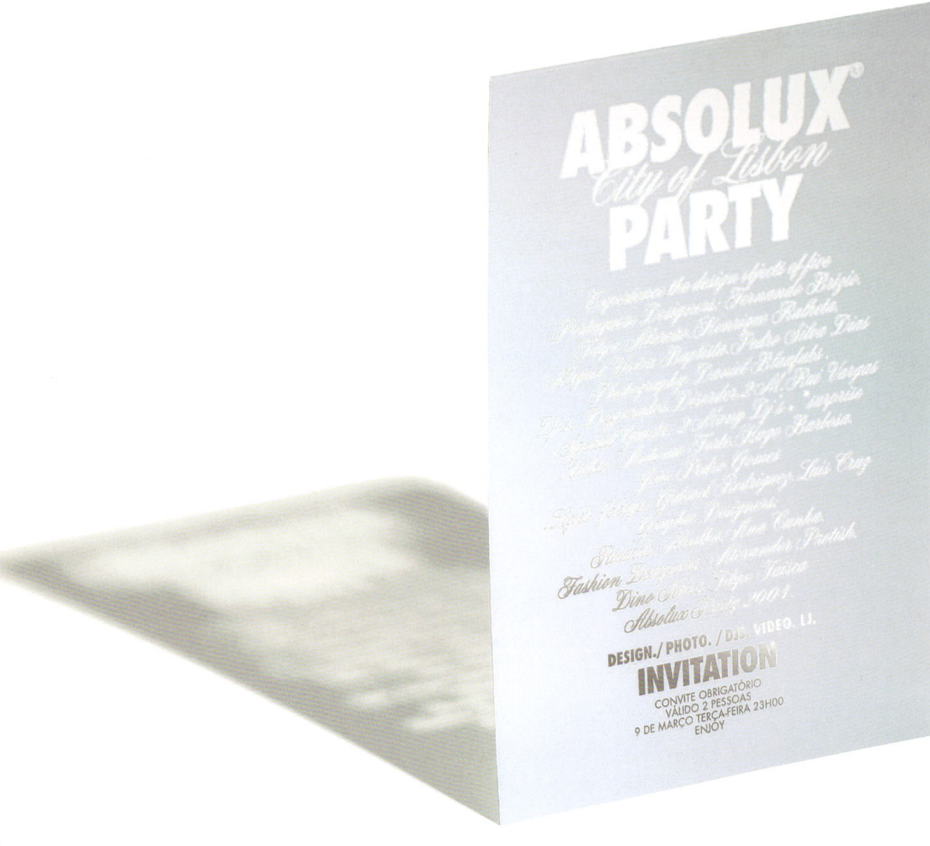

Invitations

Invitations

Party announcement on the theme of Absolut Vanilla Vodka
The main elements of this invitation were an Absolut Vanilla Vodka bottle and the vanilla flavor behind the drink. Using gradations of white and the contrast between glossy and matte surfaces, the invitations convey brightness, transparency, and sophistication. The four-color printing on mirror-finish paper carries the image of vanilla beans.

クラブ Lux Fragil の Absoluteバニラウォッカをテーマにしたパーティー案内
コンセプトは、Absoluteバニラ・ウォッカのボトルとバニラ味。白のグラデーション、グロスとマットのコントラストにより、明るさ、透明感、洗練を表現。ミラー紙にバニラビーンズのイメージを4c印刷している。

S: RMAC Brand Design　CL: Lux Fragil　CD, D: Ricardo Mealha / Ana Cunha

Invitations

Invitation to an art show, Marco 500
This is an invitation to a semiannual art show. It was designed to be an object for assembly (flower vase) because the theme was "objet." The object is made of plastic, so for the sake of the environment it is meant to be reused.

オブジェがテーマのアートショー Marco 500 へのインビテーション
年2回開かれるアートショーへの招待状。テーマが「オブジェ」だったため、組み立てるとオブジェ(花瓶)になるデザインに。プラスチックを使用しているものの、後から使えるという意味で環境面にも配慮している。

DF, S: orlando facioli design　CD, AD, D, I, P, CW: Orlando Facioli　CL: marco 500

Invitation to flower shop opening
A flower vase was recreated using cardboard as a response to two requests, one for the design of an invitation and the other for the design of a flower vase. This invitation was sent with an actual flower, which means the card itself takes advantage of the flower's attractive features.

花瓶として使える、花店のオープニング招待状
インビテーションのデザインと花瓶のデザインという2つの要望に応えるソリューションとして、板紙で花瓶を制作。このカードは花とともに送られ、花の美しさを最大限に生かすインビテーションとなった。

CD, AD, D, S: Paula Rosa　CL: Florinda

Invitations

Invitations

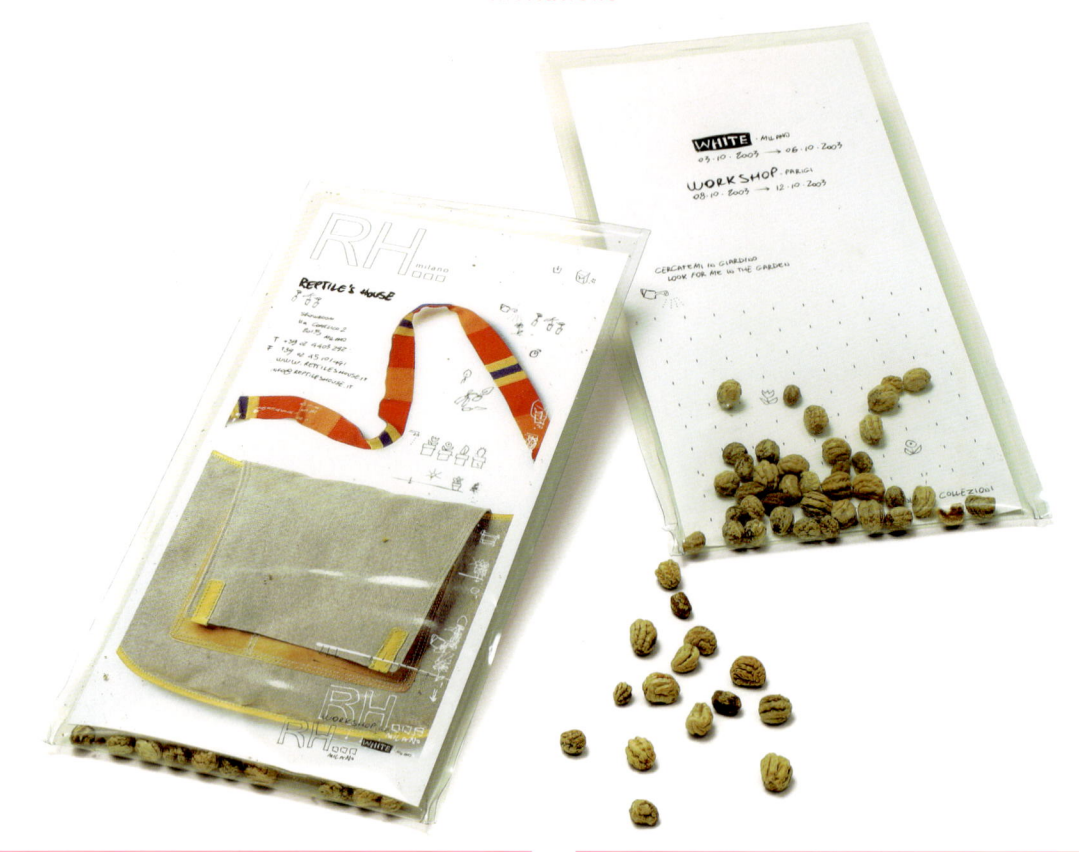

1
Invitation to a fashion exhibit
The invitation uses a gardening theme for a fashion accessories brand (bags and belts). Transparent folders contain photos of bags and real flower seeds.

ガーデニングをテーマにした、アパレルブランドの展示会案内
ファッションアクセサリー（バッグやベルト）ブランドのための、ガーデニングをテーマにしたインビテーション。透明のパッケージの中には、バッグの写真と本物の花の種が入っている。

DF, S: jekyll & hyde   CL: Reptile's House   CD: Marco Molteni / Margherita Monguzzi

Invitation to an event for direct mail companies
MOSMOS is an epoch-making direct mail idea that utilizes a transparent capsule to hold samples for distribution. MOSMOS are delivered as invitations to events that MOSMOS takes part in for the purpose of exposing people to the charms of MOSMOS so that they remain in their minds.

カプセル型DM製作会社が参加するイベントへの招待状
MOSMOSとは、透明カプセルにサンプル等を入れて送る画期的なDM。MOSMOSが参加するイベントの招待状および来店の礼状として、MOSMOSを実際に届けてその魅力を体験してもらい、記憶に留めてもらうことを狙った。

S: CIPS CO.,LTD.   CD: Mituo Ueno   AD: Yuka Otomo   D: Yukiko Yamamoto   DF: K's media CO.,LTD.

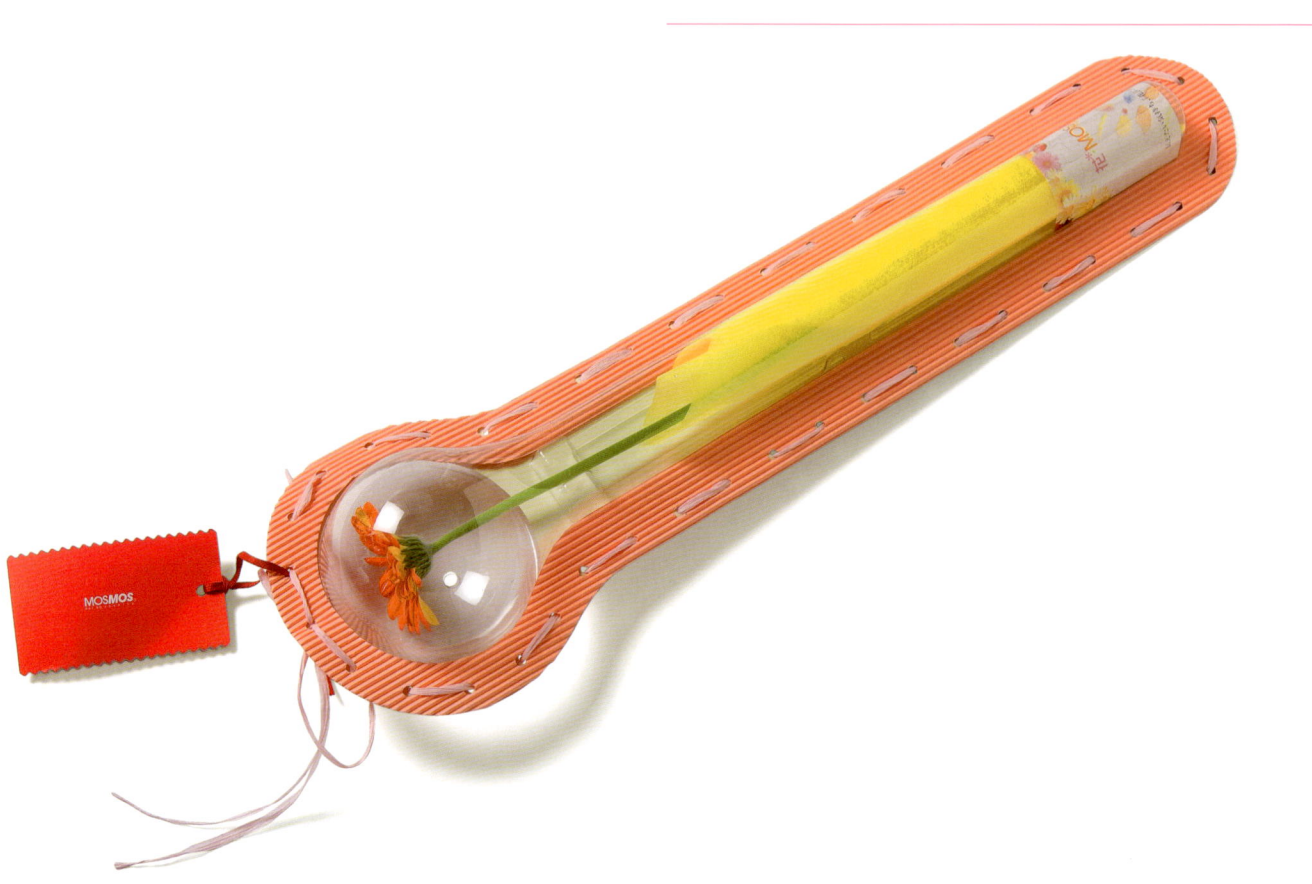

2

Greetings

Greetings

Christmas snowman kit sent out by frozen food company
This snowman box contained a carrot, walnuts, and buttons. All that was missing to make a snowman was snow. The client is a logistics server for frozen foods, so the implied message was that "We will deliver products as cold as snow".

冷凍食品を扱う物流業者が送る、クリスマスの雪だるまキット
ニンジン、くるみ、ボタンなどのパーツが入っているスノーマン・ボックス。あと足りないのは雪。依頼主は冷凍食品の管理業者であるため、雪のように冷たい商品をお届けします、というメッセージも込めている。

DF, S: Raineri Design　CL: Krio Trans

Greetings

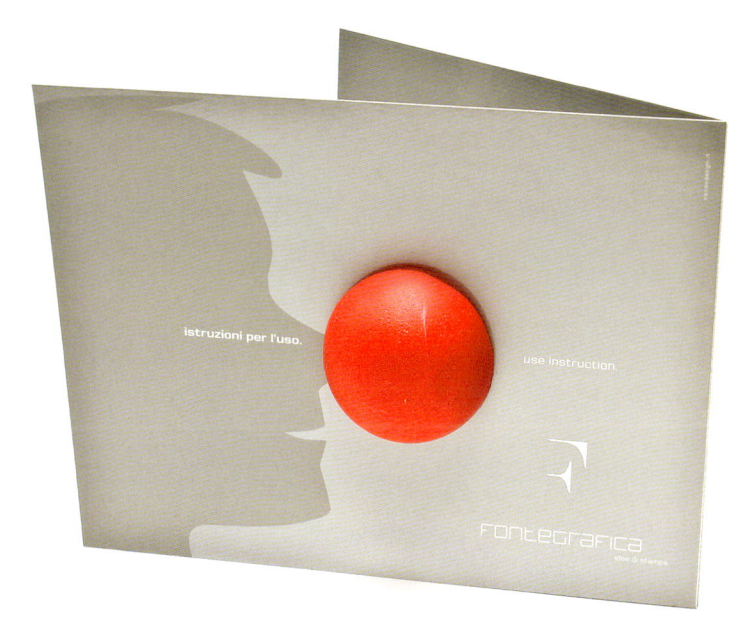

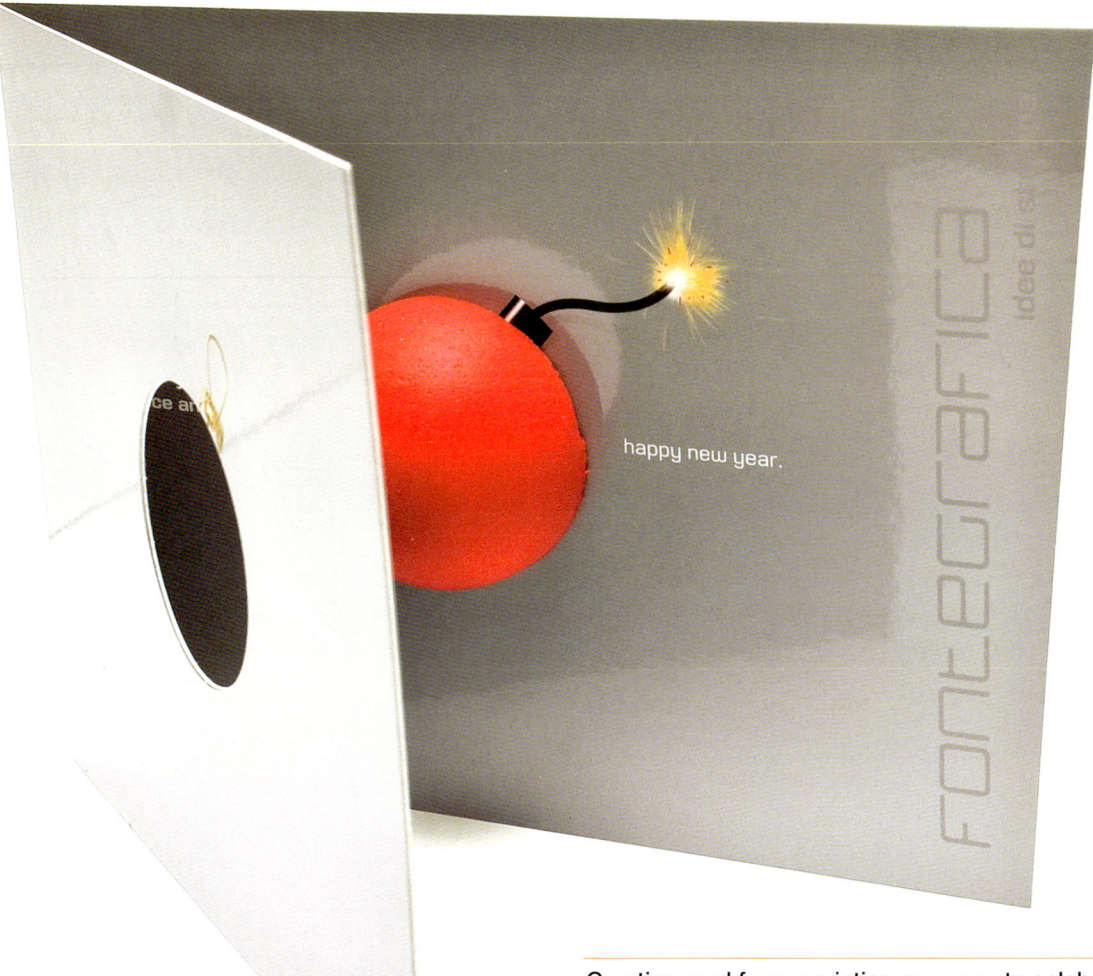

Greeting card from a printing company to celebrate the end of the year.
The company's 2008 calendar was all about David Larible, one of the world's most famous clowns, and the day the greeting cares were sent out was close to the day that the calendar would be publicly presented, so this relationship was emphasized. The red ball changes from a Christmas decoration to a bomb to a clown's nose.

ツリーの飾り、爆弾、道化の鼻になる赤い球が印象的な、印刷会社の挨拶状
同社の2008年カレンダーは世界的な道化、デービッド・ラリブルがテーマで、そのカレンダーの発表会がこの挨拶状の送付時期と近かったため、関連を持たせた。赤い球はツリーの飾り、爆弾、道化の鼻へと変わる。

DF, S: Cacao Design   CL: Fontegrafica   CD: Mauro Pastore / Masa Magnoni / Alessandro Floridia
D: Laura Salis

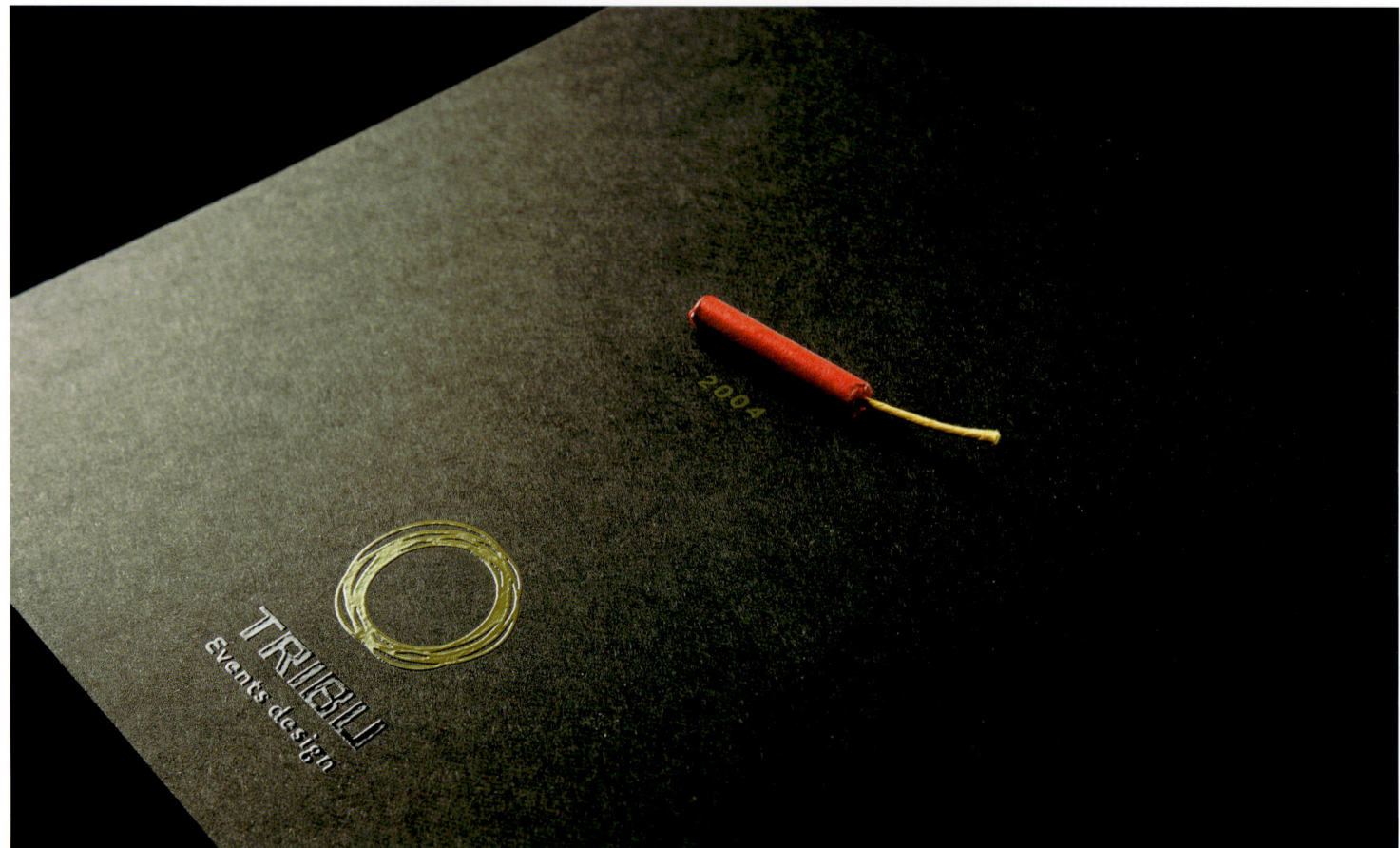

Greetings

Simple New Years card for a caterer using fireworks
This simple New Years card featured a fireworks object that is familiar to all Italians, a minimum amount of text, and the company logo. The purpose of the card was to establish a brand image using the same design as that used for the event invitation on page 52.

新年を祝う花火のオブジェを付けた、ケータリング会社のシンプルな年賀状
イタリア人なら誰もが一度は遊んだことのある定番の花火をかたどったオブジェと、最小限の文字、企業ロゴのみでまとめたシンプルな年賀状。イベント招待状（p52）と同デザインでブランド・イメージ確立を狙った。

DF, S: Cacao Design　CL: Tribu　CD: Mauro Pastore / Masa Magnoni / Alessandro Floridia
D: Paolo Sala

Greetings

Greeting card for a caterer that includes hay
Greeting card for OL3, a catering service. In order to convey maximum impact at minimum cost, were enclosed with the message "5 grams of hay, special catering for reindeer".

トナカイのための干草が付いたケータリング・サービス会社のグリーティング
ケータリング・サービスを提供するOL3の挨拶状。低コストでインパクトのあるカードにするため本物の穀物を添付し、「干草5g、トナカイのための特別なケータリング」というメッセージを添えた。

DF, S: Cacao Design   CL: OL3   CD: Mauro Pastore / Masa Magnoni / Alessandro Floridia   D: Paolo Sala

103

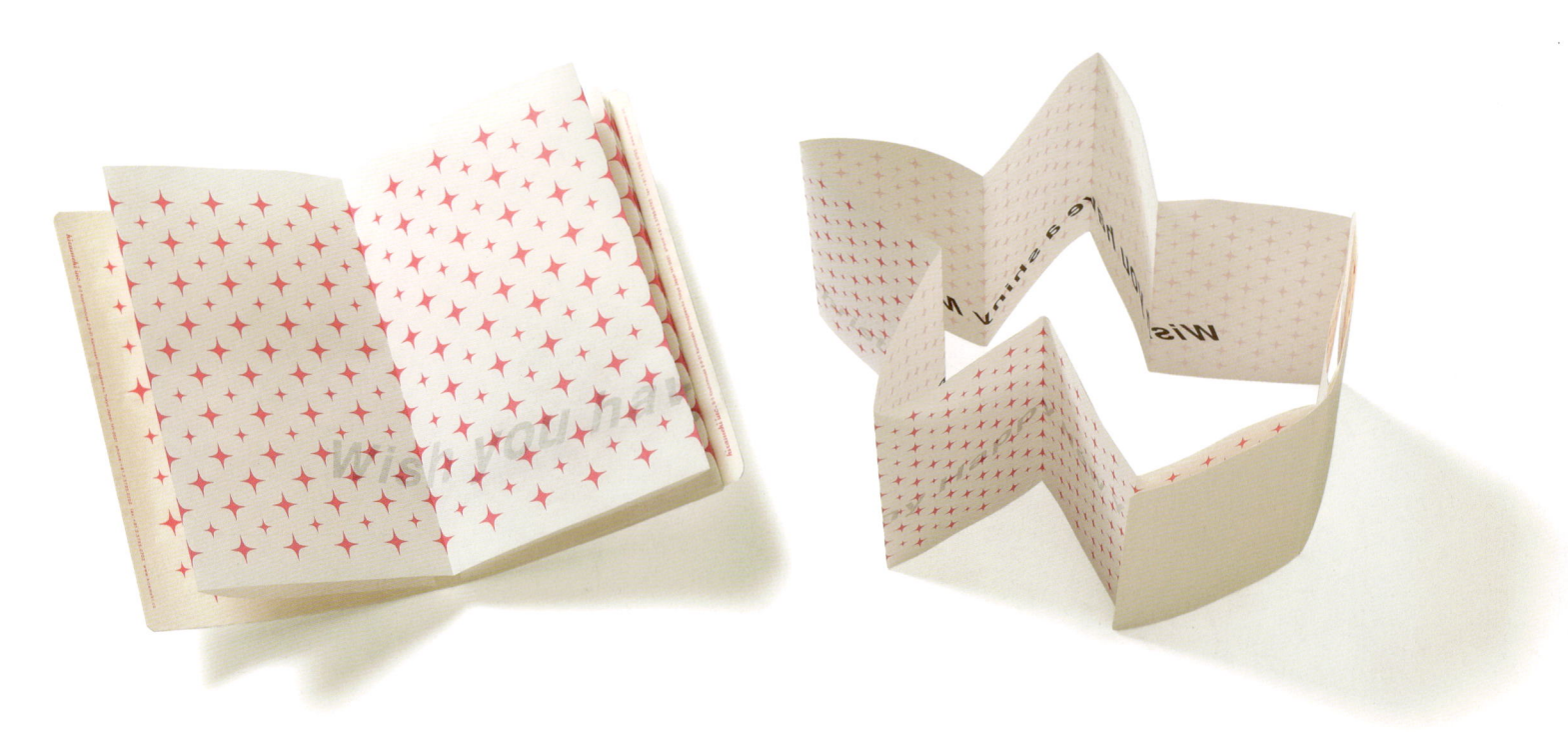

1
Seasonal greeting expressed in logos
The aim was to produce a concept book that doesn't suggest a clear concept. It was designed in such a way that the message printed inside could be seen through the envelope. Women found it very attractive.

デザイン会社のロゴで表現した、コンセプトブックのような挨拶状
明確なコンセプトを感じさせないコンセプトブックのようなものを狙った。内側に印刷されたメッセージが透けて見えるデザイン。「かわいい」と女性に人気が高かった。

S: kirameki inc.　AD: Tomohito Ushiro　D: Keisuke Yanagawa　DF: Sude　Producer: Yoshiki Ishii

2
Design company Christmas card that emphasizes a wreath
A Christmas wreath represents a warm invitation to friends. These two specially produced Christmas wreaths convey a celebratory atmosphere while also mimicking the company logo.

企業ロゴをかたどったリースがポイントの、デザイン会社のXmasカード
クリスマス・リースは、何世紀も前から、温かく友を迎え入れる歓迎のシンボル。特別に制作した2つのクリスマス・リースは、祝祭の雰囲気を伝えながら、同社のロゴをも表している。

CL, S: Circle Communications Ltd.　CD, AD, D, I: Lily Tse

Greetings

New Years card with nostalgic eyeglasses-shaped confection
Direct mail self-promotion featuring imitation eyeglasses and a lens-cleaning cloth that was sent out to commemorate Chinese New Years. The nostalgic candy packs, which come in the shape of the company logo, brings back fond memories. This direct mail conveys the clients corporate identity as well as a warm feeling.

ロゴをかたどったメガネ型お菓子が懐かしい、デザイン・スタジオの年賀状
中国の新年（旧正月）に送られた、メガネとメガネ拭きを模したPR用のDM。ロゴをかたどった昔懐かしいキャンディのパッケージは、受け取った人に優しい記憶を蘇らせる。CIと温かい気持ちをうまく表現したDM。

CL, S: Circle Communications Ltd.   CD, AD, D: Lily Tse

Greetings

Announcement card for a fire festival using a shimmering fantasy silhouette
This card was for Spain's Sant Joan Fire Festival (June 23), which takes place at a university arboretum. A portion of a hand of the figure is inserted in a slot at the top of the card, and then the card is held above a candle flame. A silhouette appears.

ゆらゆらと映し出される影が幻想的な、火祭りイベントのお知らせ
大学の植物園で行われるスペインの祝祭、サン・ホアンの火祭り(6月23日)の案内。カードの人形の手の部分を上部の穴に差し込み、ろうそくの炎にかざすと影絵のように映し出される仕組み。

DF, S: Espirelius CB　　CL: Universitat de València

Greetings

1

New Years greeting based on the concept of a "warm heart"
New Years cards used as corporate tools for tenta en lata, a design company. Teabag-shaped packages contain die-cut hearts. The message "In 2005 don't let it cool down" is written on the tag.

「温かいハートを贈る」をコンセプトにしたデザイン会社の新年の挨拶状
デザイン会社 tinta en lata の自社ツールとして制作された新年の挨拶状。ティーバッグ型のパッケージの中には、型抜きされたハート型のカードが。「温かな気持ちで」というメッセージが添えられている。

CL, S: tinta en lata   CD, AD, D: Julia Rube

New Years card with a message to "stay passionate"
New Years cards that were sent out with wishes for good business relations. Real matches are attached to the cards to directly express the message "For 2006 don't let it go out".

「心の火を絶やさずに！」というメッセージを込めたデザイン会社の年賀状
良好な取引関係を願って送られた新年の挨拶状。カードには本物のマッチが付けられており、「今年も熱く燃えて」というメッセージをストレートに表現している。

CL, S: tinta en lata   CD, AD, D: Julia Rube

2

107

Greetings

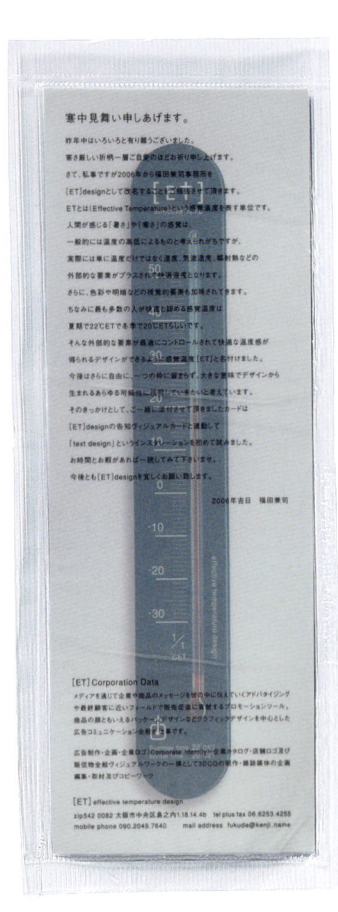

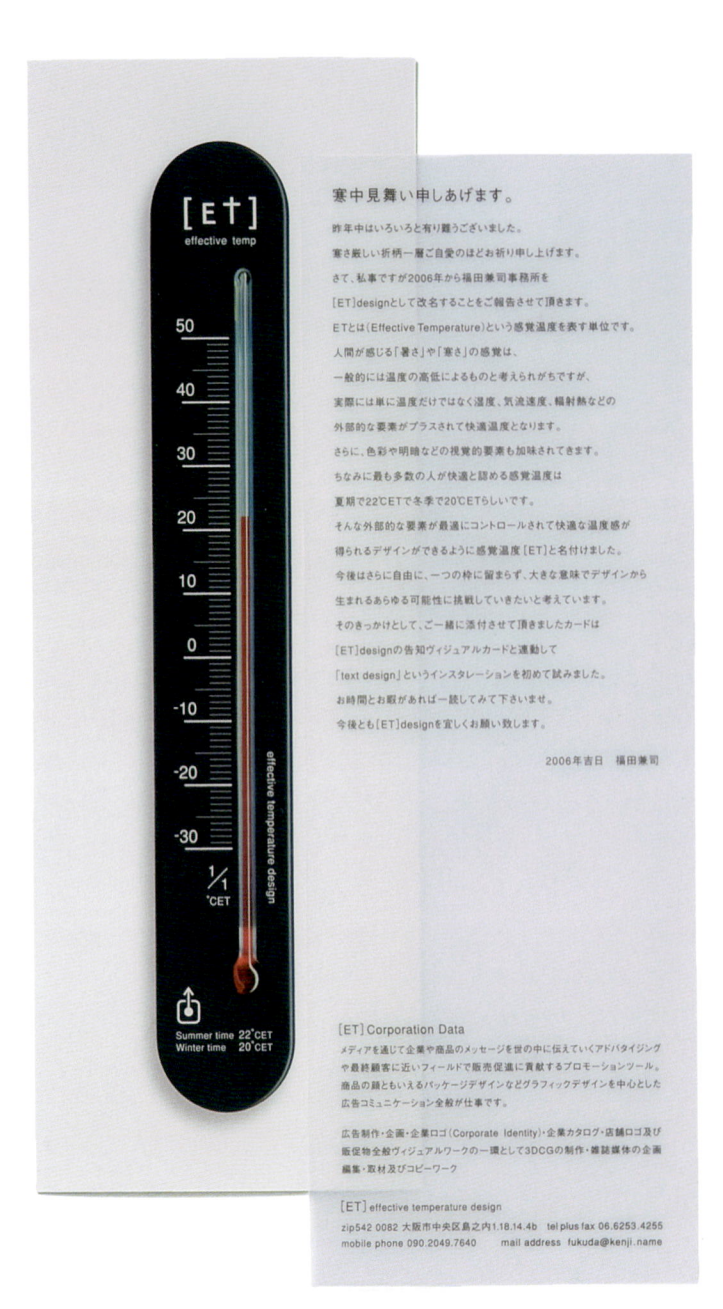

Winter greeting for a design company using heat-sensitive printing and vacuum packaging
The purpose of this direct mail is new promotion for a private office. The graphics tried to rely on text rather than on visual design. A heat-sensitive printing process and vacuum packaging were used.

示温印刷と真空パックを採用した、デザイン会社の寒中見舞い
特殊な素材や加工で、新しいプロモーションの可能性にチャレンジしたDM。ヴィジュアル・イメージだけでなく文字をデザイン要素としたグラフィックを試みている。熱を加えると色が消える示温印刷と真空パックを採用。

CL, CD, AD, D, DF, CW, S: Fukuda Kenji Graphic Design

Greetings

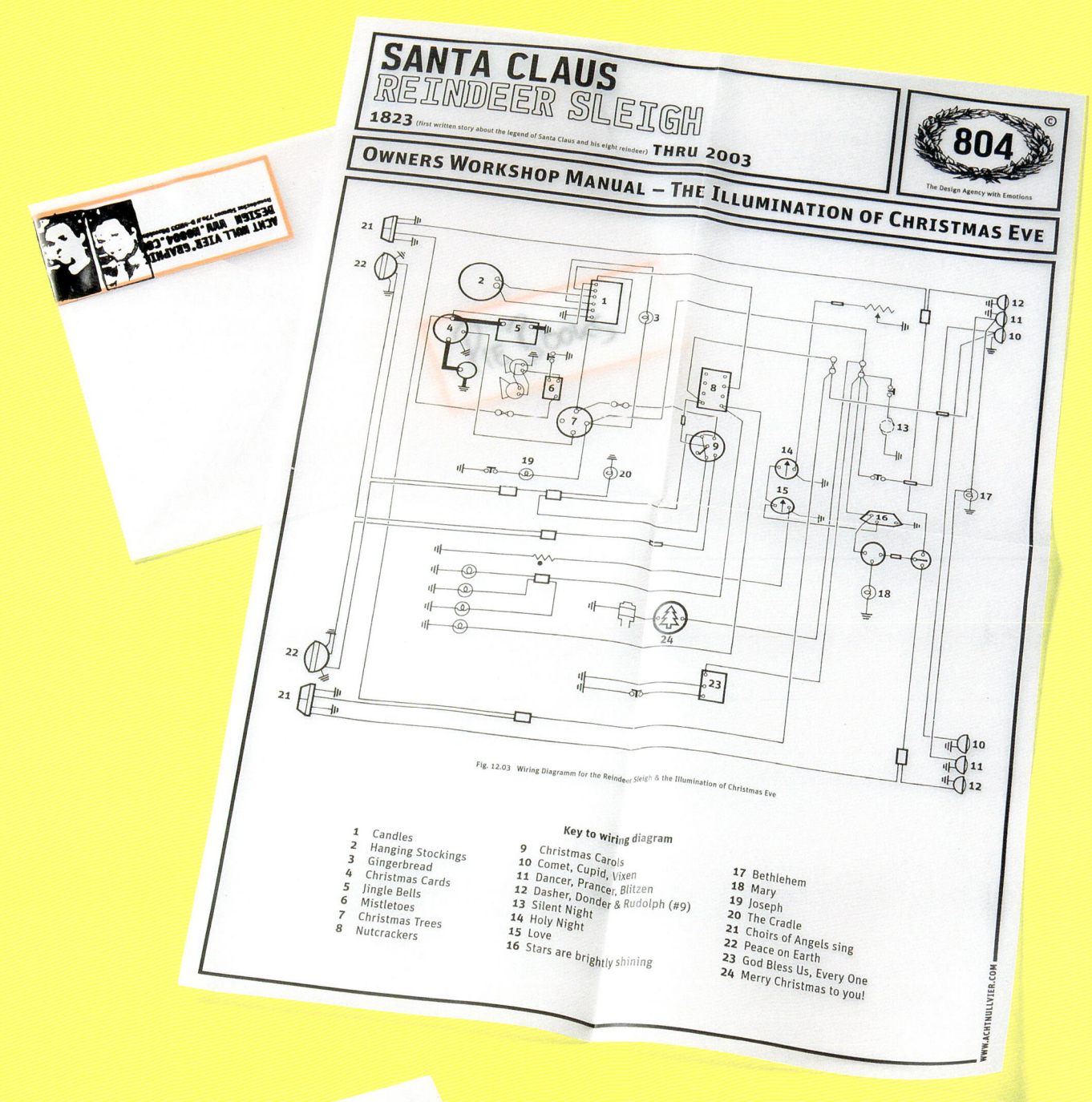

Christmas card that can be reused as wrapping paper
The basic concepts were "big impact" and "recyclable". Useful as wrapping paper, the card's purpose was to expand the network of potential clients. In the future the company plans to sell this paper on line after adding more designs.

ラッピングペーパーとして再利用できるデザイン会社のクリスマス・カード
コンセプトは「印象的で後から利用できるもの」。Xmasイルミネーションの配線図を包装紙として利用してもらうことで、顧客候補の輪が広がることを狙った。今後、種類を増やしオンライン販売も予定している。

CL, DF, S: 804©GRAPHIC DESIGN   CD: Helge Rieder / Oliver Henn

109

Greetings

1

Seasonal greeting that explains autumn and fallen leaves
This red card comes with business-related information. The printing style is letterpress. Fallen leaves are glued to the card, which also features a printed explanation of why leaves change color and how to enjoy the autumn colors in different countries. Tags are included with information about where and when the fallen leaves were collected and how long it took to dry them.

秋や紅葉にまつわるウンチクを紹介するデザイン・スタジオの季節の挨拶
赤いカードには事業に関する内容を掲載。印刷は活版を採用。落ち葉を貼ったカードには紅葉のメカニズムや各国の秋の楽しみ方が紹介されている。また、それぞれの落ち葉の採集場所や日時、乾燥にかかった時間などを記載したタグを1枚1枚貼り付けている。

CL, DF, S: Heinz Wild Design   CD, AD, D: Heinz Wild

Christmas calendar gift on the themes of time, work and freedom
People at work cross out days on a calendar like prisoners counting off the days until their release. "Work Brings Freedom" is a play on the motto of Auschwitz, and the envelope is covered with the fingerprints of the staff. On the back is a philosophical message: Life is Time, Time is Money, Is Money Life?

時間、仕事、自由をテーマにしたデザイン会社のXmasカレンダー・ギフト
釈放の日までを数える囚人のように、仕事に拘束された日を消していく。「Work brings Freedom（働けば自由に）」は、アウシュビッツでの言葉を皮肉ったもの。封筒にはスタッフの指紋、裏にはLife is Time, Time is Money, Is Money Life?という哲学的メッセージが。

DF, S: Joseph Rossi srl   D: Graphic First Aid   CL: Joseph Rossi

2

110

Greetings

Christmas cards with tags that can be used on gifts
A list of websites about holidays in different countries is printed on the wrapper. One sheet has five gift tags, each with greetings in a different language so that the recipient of the card is moved to give presents to others.

受け取った人がプレゼント・タグとして使えるデザイン会社のXmasカード
パッケージには各国の祝日に関するウェブサイトがリストアップされている。1枚のシートにはさまざまな言語で書かれたメッセージタグが5枚付いていて、受け取った人が贈り物をしたくなるようなカードに仕上がった。

CL, DF, S: Heinz Wild Design   CD, AD, D, I: Heinz Wild   I: Petra Beisse

Greetings

1

Summertime greeting for a design company
The design is simple and straightforward, featuring 13 cards wrapped in pearl-textured navy blue paper and held together by an address label, emphasizing the attractiveness of sea shells. Also enclosed is an explanation of the composition of sea water, marine animals, and the functional beauty of sea shells.

デザイン会社の知的なこだわりを伝える、海をテーマにした暑中見舞い
13枚のカードをパール感のある紺色の包装紙で包み、住所ラベルで封をし、貝殻の美しさを引き立てるシンプルでストレートなデザインを追及。海水の成分や海の生物のこと、貝殻の機能美などの説明も同封した。

CL, DF, S: Heinz Wild Design   CD, AD, D, I: Heinz Wild   P: Michael Rast   CW: Kurt Schori

New Year's greeting card
A unseasonal summer beach photo is used to provide an element of surprise. Enclosed is a business review card stating the previous year's achievements and gratitude to those who contributed to those achievements. These seasonal greetings, which started eight years ago, are sent out once or twice a year and have become collectors items.

夏の海辺の写真で意外性を狙ったデザイン会社のニューイヤーズ・カード
意外性を狙い、あえて夏の海辺の写真を採用。この年の成果と貢献者への感謝を記したビジネスレビュー・カードも同封した。8年前から年に1、2回送付している季節の挨拶状は、コレクターズアイテムになっている。

DF, S: Heinz Wild Design   CD, AD, D, P: Heinz Wild   AD, P: Daniela Zanovello   CW: Elisabeth Wild

2

112

Greetings

Christmas card that uses a high-quality printing process and paper
Using matte and glossy varnish, gold, and embossing, the client is able to express a unique world view every year. The purpose is to express something new through the choice of printing, processing and paper stock, thus creating promotional tools that convey the studio's curiosity and originality.

印刷加工・紙にこだわったXmasカードでデザイン・スタジオの世界観を表現
マットとグロスのニス、ゴールド、エンボスなどを採用し、毎年ユニークな世界観を表現。印刷、加工、用紙にこだわり、新しい表現を追求することで、スタジオの好奇心や独創性を伝える販促ツールとなっている。

CL, DF, S: SCANDINAVIAN DESIGNLAB　CD, D: Per Madsen

Greetings

Christmas tree greeting card that can double as a decoration
The perfect Christmas tree for a single person living alone, it can be hung on the wall using seals. The poster, made of recycled paper, comes with three sets of colored glitter mark stickers. It received high marks, especially from children.

貼って飾れるクリスマスツリーのグリーティング
シールを貼って自分で飾れる、一人暮らしにも便利なクリスマス・ツリー。再生紙のポスターに3色のキラメキマークのステッカーが付いている。かなり評判が良く、子どもにも喜ばれた。

S: kirameki inc.　AD: Tomohito Ushiro　D: Keisuke Yanagawa　P: Naoki Hashimoto　DF: Sude

Greetings

1

Christmas greeting that allows recipients to customize their wishes
This interactive greeting card features a white space with the words "We Wish You...", which the recipient can complete by applying words written on seals onto the card.

願い事をカスタマイズできるインテリア・デザイン会社のXmasカード
受け取った人が、「We Wish You（あなたに…がもたらされますように）」と書かれた白いカードに、自分の好きな言葉のシールを貼って文章を完成させる、インタラクティブなグリーティング・カード。

DF, S: Joseph Rossi srl　CL: Cariolato　D: Graphic First Aid

Christmas greeting that allows recipients to customize a message
This is a greeting from Roberto Valerio. On the front of the card is the message, "We Would Like to Wish You..", while inside the card phrases such as "a good year", "peace and serenity", and "good job" are positioned in such a way that the recipient can check off any one he or she desires.

受け取った人が好きな言葉を選べるクリスマス・カード
Roverto Valerioのグリーティング。「あなたに…がもたらされますように」と書かれたカードの内側には、「よい年」「平和と健康」「よい仕事」などの項目が並び、好きな言葉を選ぶことができる。

DF, S: Joseph Rossi srl　CL: Roberto Valerio　D: Graphic First Aid

2

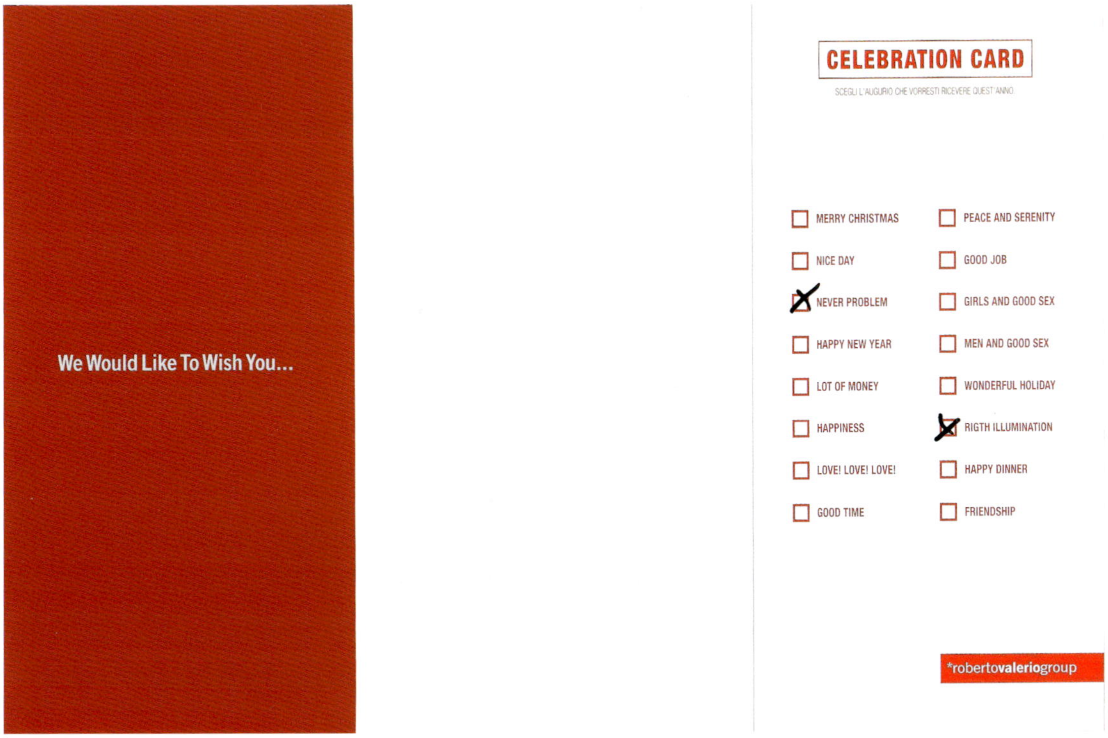

115

Greetings

Christmas card whose design transcends national borders and languages
These Christmas cards were produced by the Museum of Modern Art in New York and sold in various countries throughout the world. The purpose of the design is to convey a message that transcends languages and national borders and stresses the joy of Christmas and the bonds of family.

国や言葉を超えて伝わるデザインを狙ったXmasカード
ニューヨーク近代美術館との製作により、世界各国で発売されているクリスマス・カード。クリスマスの楽しさ、家族との絆といったメッセージが言葉や国境を越えて伝わるデザインを狙った。

AD, D, I, S: Keisuke Unosawa　CL: The Museum of Modern Art　DF: OPERA Inc.

Greetings

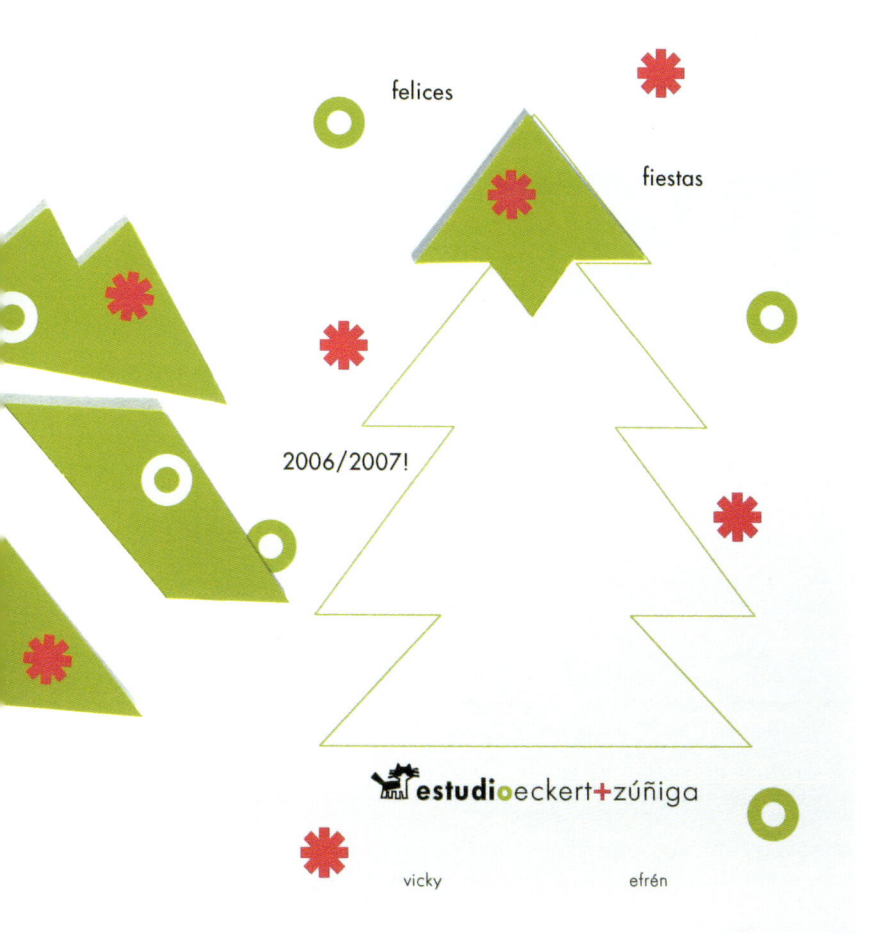

Provocative Christmas puzzle tree from a design company
A Christmas card in jigsaw puzzle form that changes the mood of the recipient. It looks simple, but it isn't. It provokes the recipient's curiosity. Anyone can enjoy it by competing with other to see who can finish it first.

思わずやってみたくなる、デザイン会社のXmasパズルツリー
ちょっとした気分転換に、思わず挑戦したくなるパズル式のクリスマス・カード。シンプルだが見た目ほど簡単でないところが、さらに興味を掻き立てる。誰が早くできるか競争したりと、みんなで楽しめる。

CL, S: Estudio Eckert+Zuniga   CD: Vicky Eckert   AD: Efren Zuniga

117

Greetings

Christmas gift from a design studio with an image of a winter forest
A Christmas gift for friends and clients. Enclosed is a scented pine cone and pine needles. The idea was to make scented objects that could be displayed on the recipient's desk just like Christmas cards.

冬の森をイメージした、デザイン・スタジオのクリスマス・ギフト
友人やクライアントに向けたクリスマス・ギフト。香りを付けた松ボックリと葉っぱを同封。机の上に飾ることができる、クリスマスらしいオブジェ十香りを届けるグリーティングに仕上がった。

DF, S: Tupos Design Company   CD, AD, D, I: Iris Kwok   CD: Gabriel Tsang   I: Elaine Chiu

Greetings

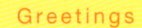

Christmas card whose design transcends national borders and languages
These Christmas cards were produced by the Museum of Modern Art in New York and sold in various countries throughout the world. The purpose of the design is to convey a message that transcends languages and national borders and stresses the joy of Christmas and the bonds of family.

国や言葉を超えて伝わるデザインを狙ったXmasカード
ニューヨーク近代美術館との製作により、世界各国で発売されているクリスマス・カード。クリスマスの楽しさ、家族との絆といったメッセージが言葉や国境を越えて伝わるデザインを狙った。

AD, D, I, S: Keisuke Unosawa   CL: The Museum of Modern Art   DF: OPERA Inc.

Greetings

Christmas card whose design transcends national borders and languages
These Christmas cards were produced by the Museum of Modern Art in New York and sold in various countries throughout the world. The purpose of the design is to convey a message that transcends languages and national borders and stresses the joy of Christmas and the bonds of family.

国や言葉を超えて伝わるデザインを狙ったXmasカード
ニューヨーク近代美術館との製作により、世界各国で発売されているクリスマス・カード。クリスマスの楽しさ、家族との絆といったメッセージが言葉や国境を越えて伝わるデザインを狙った。

AD, D, I, S: Keisuke Unosawa　CL: The Museum of Modern Art　DF: OPERA Inc.

1

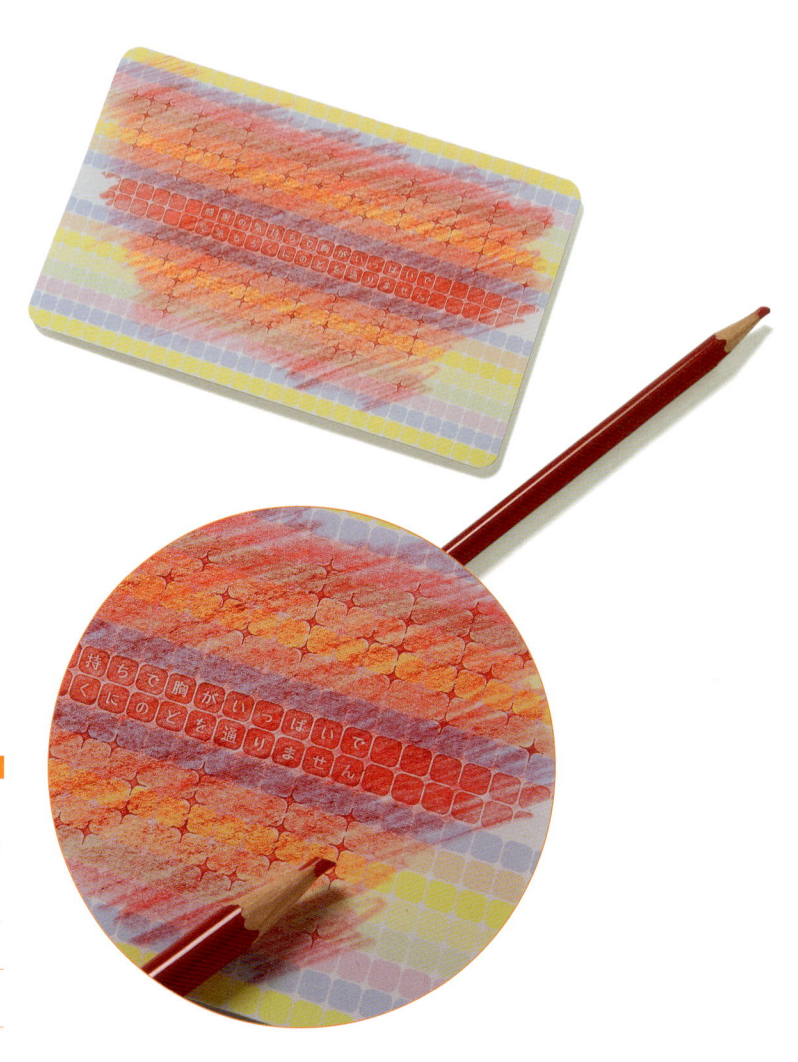

Card where words appear when the surface is rubbed
This birthday or thank you card includes a latent message. Friction printing was used so that when rubbing the surface with pen or pencil a picture appears. The card was designed to convey the idea of graffiti along the margins of a notebook.

上から塗ると隠された言葉が現れるメッセージ・カード
バースデーやThank youなどのメッセージにプラスαの気持ちを忍ばせたカード。鉛筆などで塗ると図像が出てくるフリクション印刷を使用。ノートに落書きする感覚をイメージしたデザインに。

DF, S: SUN-AD CO.,LTD.　CL: LABCLIP　AD, D: Miwa Akabane　CW: Rei Naito

2

Greetings

1

Christmas card based on the movie "It's a Wonderful Life"
The designer included a golden bell on a string that is threaded through an angel-shaped hole. It was inspired by the line, "Whenever you hear a bell rings an angel gets his wings," which is from the movie by the Italian-American director Frank Capra. The brand of paper used was Polyedra, made in Italy.

映画『It's a wonderful life』からヒントを得たクリスマスカード
イタリア系アメリカ人監督フランク・キャプラの映画の一節「ベルが鳴るたびに天使は羽を得る」からインスピレーションを受け、天使型の穴にゴールドの鈴を付けた。イタリアの紙ブランドPolyedraの用紙を使用。

DF, S: Studio Grafico Fez s.n.c   CL: Padoan Vernici   CD, AD, D: Massimo Breda
AD, CW: Monica Brugnera

Useful Christmas card from an interior furnishings chain store
The numbers 1, 25, and 31 are highlighted on the ruler to emphasize, respectively, New Year's Day, Christmas, and New Year's Eve. Christmas motifs were cut out of the ruler using lasers so that they could be used as stencils.

インテリア・デザイン会社の「使える」クリスマス・カード
定規の目盛りは1（元旦）、25（クリスマス）、31（大晦日）の数字が強調されている。ステンシルの型としても使ってもらえるよう、クリスマスのモチーフがレーザーで型抜きされている。

DF, S: Joseph Rossi srl   CL: Cariolato   D: Graphic First Aid

2

Christmas card from a design studio using cute reindeer figures
Christmas cards for a graphic design studio. The motif is a funny reindeer celebrating a merry Christmas. The handmade puppet was produced by Anna Mainenti, a friend of the design company.

デザイン・スタジオが制作したかわいいトナカイ人形のXmasカード
グラフィック・デザイン・スタジオのクリスマス・カード。ハッピークリスマスを祝うおかしなトナカイがモチーフ。手製の人形は友人であるアンナ・マイネッティが制作したもの。

CL, DF, S: Happycentro+Sintetik   CD, AD, D: Federico Galvani   D, I: Anna Mainenti

Greetings

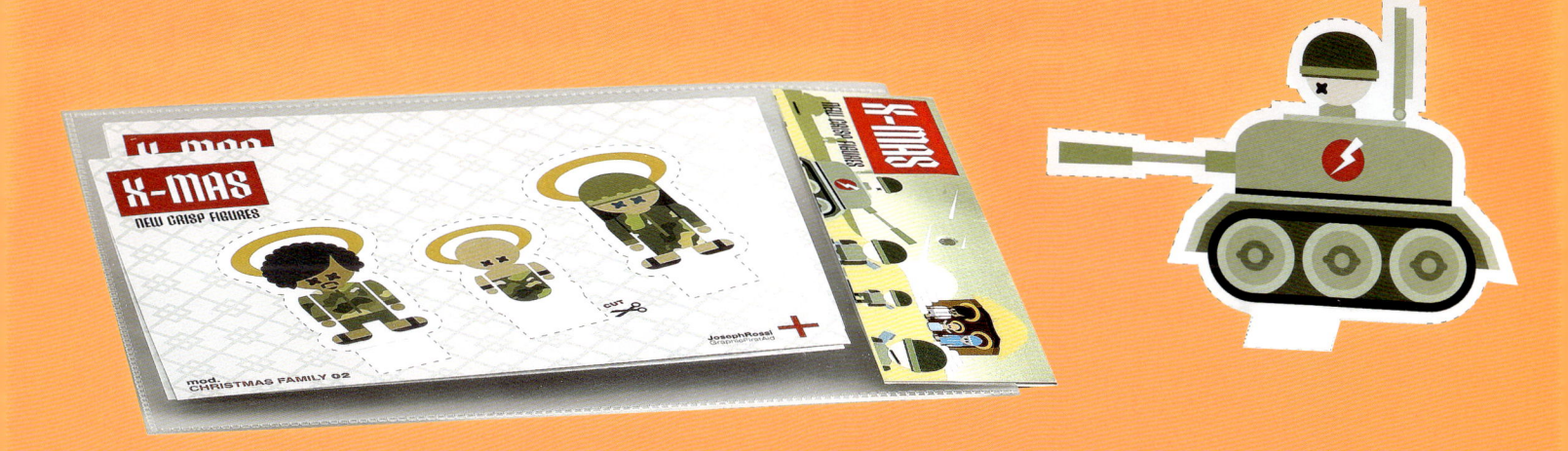

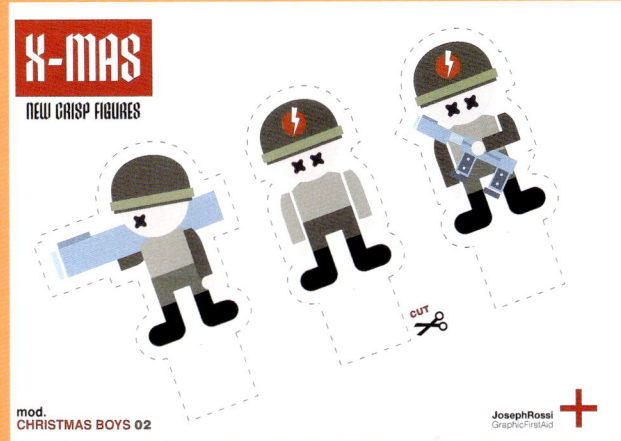

Cynical Christmas card to promote world peace
Christmastime is not necessarily an enjoyable season for everyone. There are political and religious conflicts taking place even in the Holy Land. In this kit, the Holy Family are in uniform and the shepherds are in tanks. They can be cut out and removed. It represents the tragedy of war.

世界平和を訴えるシニカルなクリスマス・カード
クリスマスに誰もが楽しい時間を過ごしているとは限らず、聖地でさえ、政治・宗教戦争が繰り広げられている。軍服を着た聖なる家族や戦車に乗った牧師を切り取って組み立てられるキットで、戦争の悲劇を訴えている。

DF, S: Joseph Rossi srl   D: Graphic First Aid   CL: Joseph Rossi

Greetings

Sophisticated Christmas card that utilizes the texture of the materials
This elegant card takes advantage of paper that turns transparent when heat is applied. PACHICA paper was used. (The envelope is Classico Tracing) The textures of the nappy material and the foil stamping make for an interesting contrast. Adults appreciated the design, and men were likely to purchase it.

起毛素材と箔押しの対比が面白い、クールなデザインのクリスマス・カード
熱を加えると透ける紙の特性を利用したエレガントなカード。使用した用紙はパチカ(封筒はクラシコトレーシング)。もうひとつは、起毛素材と箔押しの質感の対比が面白い。男性でも買いやすい大人っぽいデザイン。

S: ART PRINT JAPAN Co.,Ltd.　CD, AD, D: Asuka Nozawa

124

Greetings

Three-dimensional cards with a Christmas mood
Through a combination of transparent sheets a feeling of depth was created; while the holographic foil adds elegance. The designer has the patent for this particular form. This box-shaped greeting card expanded the world of Christmas because the white portion in the front is reflected on the silver paper background.

透明パッケージの中にXmasの世界が広がる立体的なカード
透明シートとの組み合わせで奥行きを出し、ホロ箔で高級感をプラス。この形状は特許を取得している。また、箱型のグリーティングは、背面のシルバー紙に手前の白いパーツが写りこみクリスマスの世界が広がって見える。

S: ART PRINT JAPAN Co.,Ltd.　CD, AD, D: Chikae Kobayashi

Greetings

1

Address card that looks like merchandise using hot stamping on thick chipboard
This announcement of a new address followed the relocation of Cap Rocket. Stressing texture and impact, the designer used hot stamping on very thick chipboard paper. More than just a relocation announcement, the invitation doubles as a form of merchandise.

超厚手のチップボールに箔押しでグッズ感を出したアドレスカード
CAP、ROCKETの移転に伴う新住所の案内。手触りやインパクトを重視し、超厚手のチップボール紙に箔押し。ただの引越し案内状というより、グッズ感を出すことを狙った。

CL, DF, S: CAP Inc.　AD: Yasushi Fujimoto　D: Hiromi Fujita

Christmas card for SINV
This Christmas card was made for SINV, an Italian apparel retailer. By pulling the lower tab down the Christmas tree expressed as red spots vanishes and a message appears in dots of blue, the color of the brand itself.

タブを引くと穴からメッセージが現れる、アパレルブランドのXmasカード
イタリアのアパレル製造販売業者SINVのクリスマスカード。タブを下方向に引くと、赤いドットで表現されたクリスマスツリーが消え、ブランドのテーマカラーである青のドットとともに、メッセージが表れる仕組み。

DF, S: Joseph Rossi srl　CL: SINV　D: Graphic First Aid

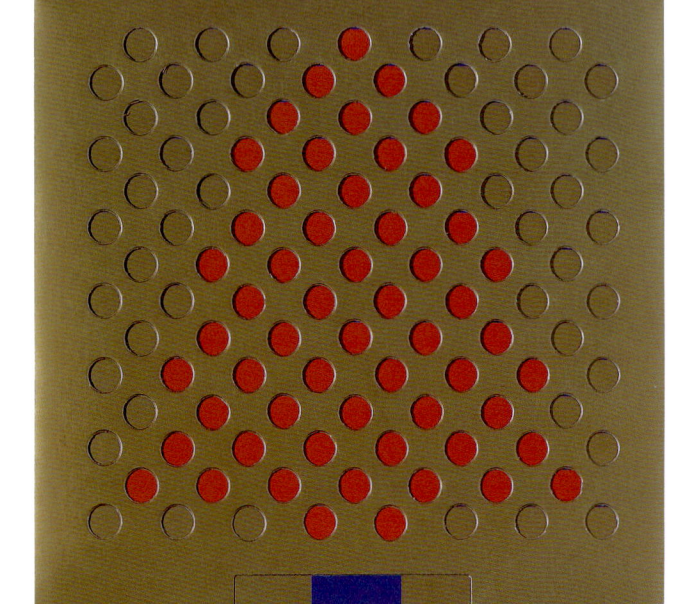

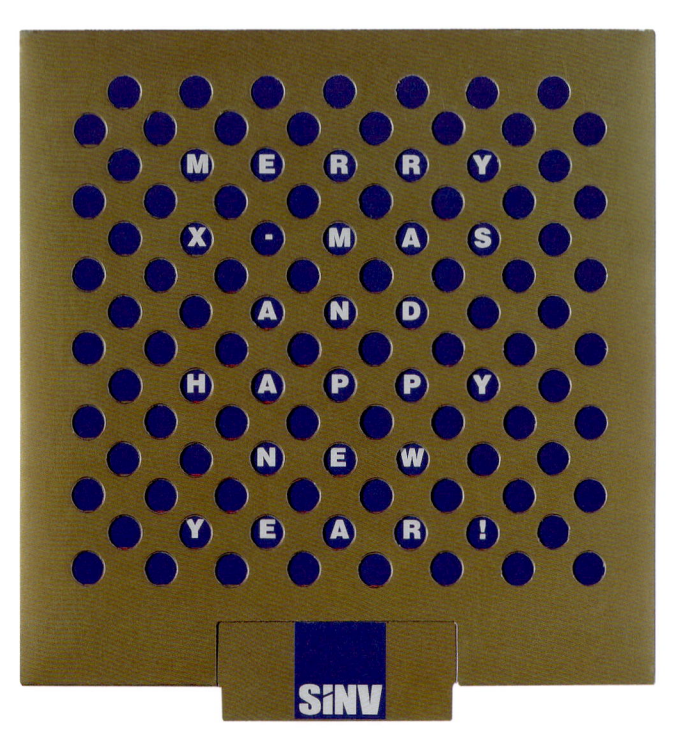

2

Greetings

1

Christmas card with a sign everyone knows
This Christmas card was designed for SINV, an Italian apparel maker and retailer. Inspired by a famous symbol of Hollywood, the design displays wit by changing the letters HOLLYWOOD to HOLIDAYS.

誰もが知っているサインをモチーフにしたクリスマス・カード
イタリアのアパレル製造販売SINVのクリスマス・カード。ハリウッドのシンボルからインスピレーションを得て、「Hollywood」の文字をHOLIDAYSに変えたウィットに富んだデザイン。

DF, S: Joseph Rossi srl   CL: SINV   D: Graphic First Aid

Valentine's Day card on the theme of murder
Valentine's Day celebrates lovers, but at the same time it was a day when Al Capone carried out a famous massacre in Chicago in the 1930s. By approaching the day from a different angle, the card takes a brutal episode as its theme and thus presents something totally unexpected.

大量殺戮をテーマにしたバレンタインデー・カード
バレンタインデーは恋人たちの祝日であると同時に、30年代のシカゴで起きたアル・カポネによる大量殺戮の日でもある。物事を別の角度から見る試みとして、この残虐な事件をテーマにしてしまった意外性に富んだ作品。

DF, S: Joseph Rossi srl   D: Graphic First Aid   CL: Joseph Rossi

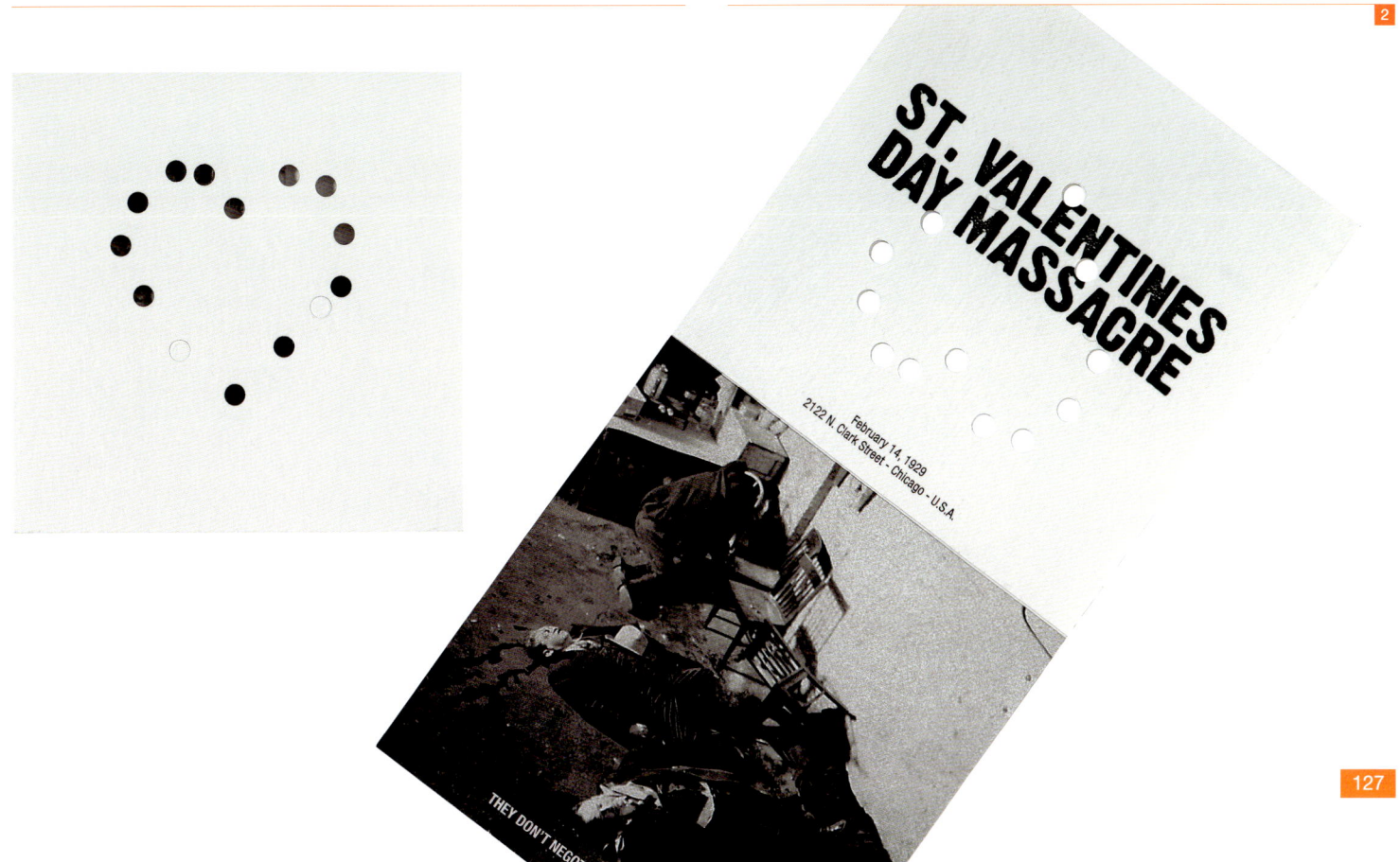

2

127

Greetings

Gift of a roll of film to promote a photo studio
A Christmas greeting sent by a photo studio to business acquaintances and prospective clients. The unique roll of film containing images of Christmas promoted technology and taste. Current business acquaintances as well as prospective clients enjoyed the idea.

オリジナルフィルムのXmasギフトで写真スタジオの技術とセンスをアピール
写真スタジオが、取引先、顧客候補に送ったクリスマスの挨拶状。クリスマスらしいイメージを焼き付けたオリジナル・フィルムで技術やセンスをアピール。従来の取引先はもちろん、新規顧客にも好評だった。

S: Roberto Trevino Design   CL: Estudio Focus   CD, AD, D, CW: Roberto Trevino   D: Ana Balen Vazquez
P: Nacho Trevino

Greetings

Winter holiday greeting card
The client wanted to create an original greeting card and utilized a coaster shape. At the planning stage they decided to send one coaster (along with a bottle of wine to preferred customers), but once they saw the design decided instead to send sets of four to all recipients. The silk screening is done by hand within the company.

不動産会社が送る、冬のグリーティング（コースター4枚セット）
依頼主が今までにない挨拶状を希望し、コースター型に。企画段階では1枚ずつ送付する（上顧客にはワインと共に送る）予定だったが、完成を見て、4枚セットで送ることに。シルクスクリーンはデザイン会社の手作業。

DF, S: Dotzero Design　CL: Davis Agency　D, I: Karen Wippich / Jon Wippich

Greetings

Valentine's Day card on the theme of tragic lovers
This Valentine's Day card was produced the year after Dody Al Fayed and Princess Diana died in a car accident. Black was used to convey mourning. Dody and Diana were chosen to be lovers of the year and their names printed in a cross.

悲運の恋人をテーマにしたバレンタインデー・カード
ドディ・アルファイド氏とダイアナ元皇太子妃が交通事故で亡くなった翌年に作られたバレンタインデーのカード。哀悼の意を込めて黒を使用。彼らを「Lovers of the Year」に選びクロスの中に記した。

DF, S: Joseph Rossi srl   D: Graphic First Aid   CL: Joseph Rossi

1

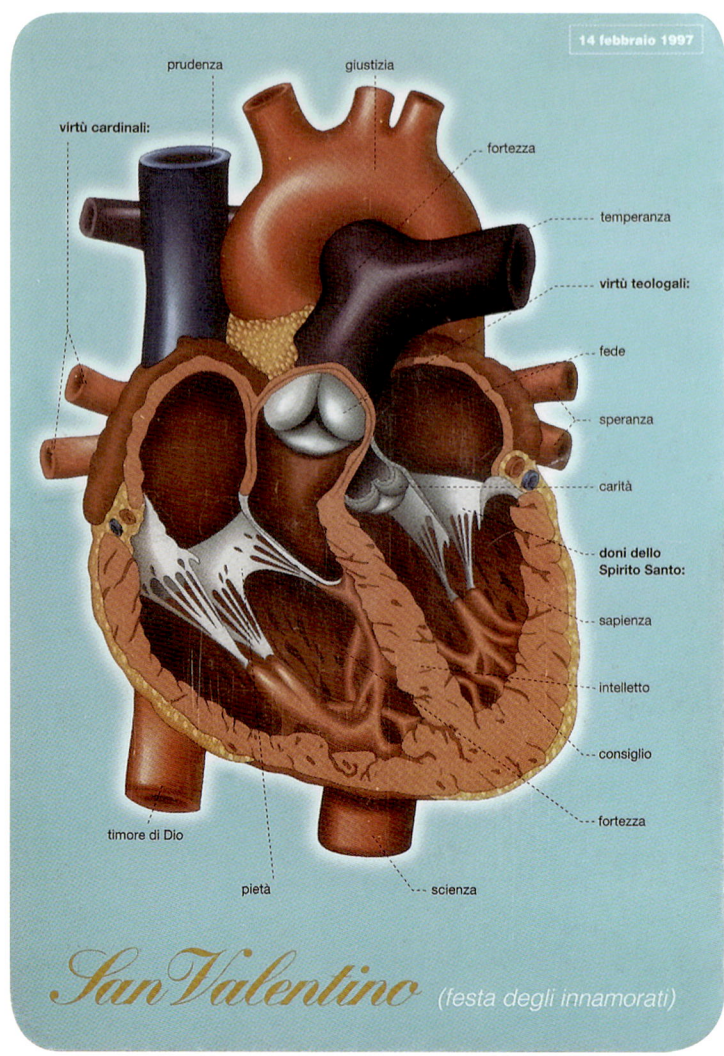

Surrealistic Valentine's Day card
This card is the antithesis of the type that celebrates Valentine's Day as a sweet occasion. An anatomical drawing of a human heart was used rather than the usual heart symbol, but the descriptions are of cardinal and spiritual virtues like "good will," "faith" and "hope," not arteries and veins.

デザイン・スタジオのウィットが光る、シュールなバレンタインデー・カード
スイートなバレンタインのイメージとはかけ離れたカード。ハートマークの代わりに心臓の解剖図を採用しているが、静脈や動脈といった解説ではなく、「善意」「信念」「希望」など神秘的な説明が付いている。

DF, S: Joseph Rossi srl   D: Graphic First Aid   CL: Joseph Rossi

2

Greetings

Christmas card that breaks with the holiday's sacred image
This naughty greeting card has a pornographic nuance, utilizing a provocative illustration and adding two more X's to Xmas, the idea being that "Christmas isn't the way it used to be."

既存の聖なるイメージを打ち破るクリスマス・カード
「クリスマスはもうこれまでのものとは違う」X-masにXをふたつ加え、挑発的なイラストを採用してポルノグラフィックな意味をもたせたノーティーなグリーティング・カード。

DF, S: Joseph Rossi srl　　D: Graphic First Aid　　CL: Joseph Rossi

1

2

Greeting card for International Women's Day (Mar. 8)
There was a case in Italy where judges acquitted an accused rapist because they said jeans cannot be removed without the cooperation of the person wearing them. This card conveys a strong message by challenging that opinion.

デザイン・スタジオが問いかける、国際女性デー（3月8日）のメッセージ
イタリアの裁判で、「ジーンズは本人の協力がないと脱がせることはできない」としてレイプ犯が無罪判決となったケースがあった。この裁判の是非を問うメッセージ色の強いカード。

DF, S: Joseph Rossi srl　　D: Graphic First Aid　　CL: Joseph Rossi

131

Greetings

1

2

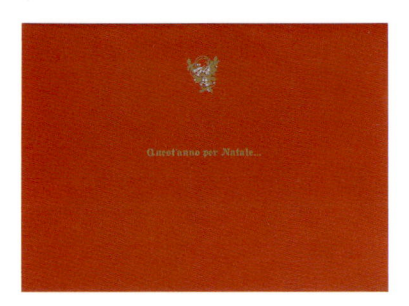

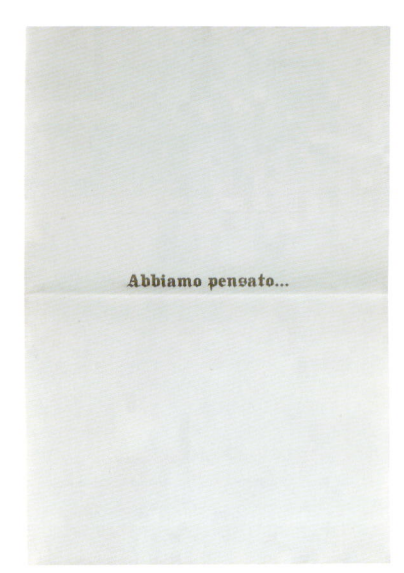

Large format Christmas greeting
The theme is "big," so a large format was used. When the greeting is opened and spread out, the pinup photo of a woman appears to be almost life-size. This sexy female motif was used for the following year's Christmas greeting but in a different form.

巨大フォーマットで送るクリスマス・グリーティング
テーマは「BIG」。広げると、ピンナップ写真の女性はほぼ実物大という、大きなフォーマットを採用した。セクシーな女性のモチーフはこの翌年のカードにも別の形で採用された。

DF, S: Joseph Rossi srl　CL: Roberto Valerio　D: Graphic First Aid

A Christmas card that's a little sexy
The client, Roberto Valerio, decided to continue using a sexy motif that had been well received in previous years. When you look at the card closely the snowflakes are revealed to be silhouettes of women's figure. Hot gold printing was used for the stars and lettering.

女性のシルエットでできた雪の結晶がセクシーなクリスマス・カード
依頼主であるRoberto Valerioは、この前年に好評を得たこのセクシーなモチーフを引き続き採用することに決定。雪の結晶をよく見ると、女性のシルエットになっている。星と文字には金箔押しを使用。

DF, S: Joseph Rossi srl　CL: Roberto Valerio　D: Graphic First Aid

Others

Others

Invitation to 3rd anniversary party-cum-relocation announcement
The illustration of a woman was used because the office's interior design was based on a kitchen motif. 3D printing was used for the illusion of space. Custom-made cardboard and shrinkpacking was also used. Because of the favorable response, the invitation was covered by magazines.

３Ｄ印刷で事務所が立体的に見える設立3周年パーティーの招待状と移転案内
キッチンをモチーフに設計した事務所にちなんで婦人のイラストを使用。空間を体験してもらえるよう3D印刷を採用した。オリジナルで作った段ボールを台紙にシュリンクパック。反響が大きく雑誌等でも紹介された。

S: kirameki inc.　CD, AD: Tomohito Ushiro　D: Kuniharu Yosehara　P: Hideyuki Takahashi　DF: Sude
Producer: Yoshiki Ishii

Others

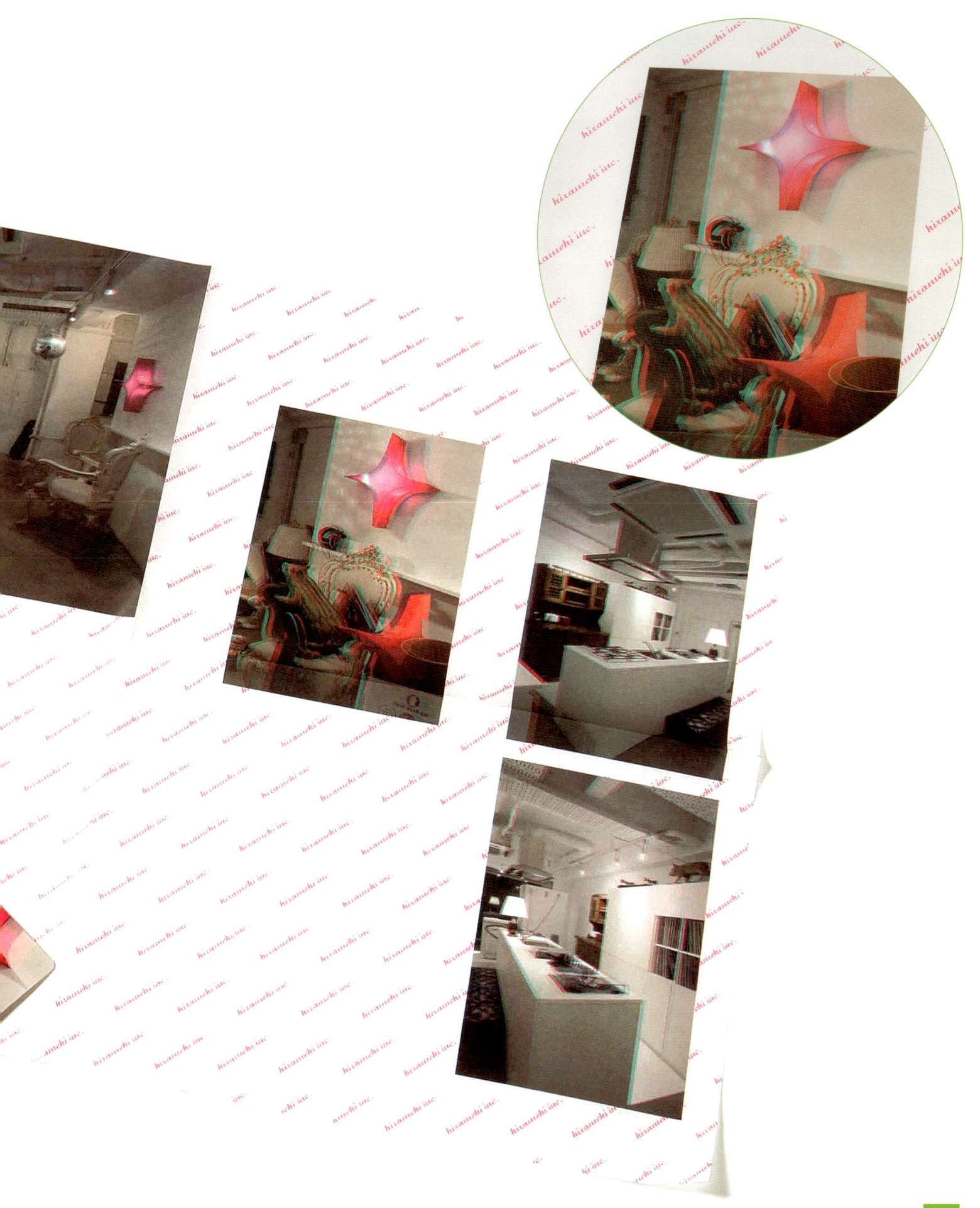

Others

Pop wedding invitation using a collage of media
The client requested humorous and informal invitations. The designer produced invitations with an ironic take on gender-role reversal by combining wallpaper and a metal plate, and then taking photographs of it for a pop touch.

壁紙、プレート、新郎新婦の写真をコラージュしたポップな結婚式の招待状
依頼主が、形式張らないユーモアのある招待状を希望していたため、男女の役割の逆転を皮肉った一風変わったカードを制作。壁紙やメタルプレートを組み合わせ、写真に撮ってポップな感じに仕上げた。

S: Roberto Trevino Design   CL, CW: Santiago Uribe   CD, AD, D: Roberto Trevino   D: Ana Balen Vazquez
P: Nacho Trevino

Others

Announcement for exhibition and wedding with a treasure map motif

The theme is wedding pirates. The announcement contains simultaneously a notification for an exhibition of Ippei Takei's brand and a notice about his wedding. The destination indicated in the treasure map is "happiness". People were very pleased with the clear concept and the response was very positive.

海賊の宝の地図をモチーフにした、ブランドの展示会＋結婚式の案内状

テーマは「パイレーツ・オブ・ウェディング」。ippei takeiブランドの展示会告知と自身の結婚式を重ねた案内状。宝の地図に示された場所は「幸福」。明確なコンセプトが喜ばれ、反響も大きかった。

CD, AD, D, DF, S: Fukuda Kenji Graphic Design　　CL: Escapes

Others

Marketing campaign for event planning and PR company
An anniversary kit sent out by an event planning company to clients who are celebrating either their 25th or 50th anniversary. At the same time this gift suggests that the client hold a commemorative event that the company can plan and produce. The box can be opened two ways and contains confetti, candles, and a music box that plays "Happy Birthday".

イベント企画・PR会社のマーケティング・キャンペーン
イベント会社が顧客の25周年、50周年に送るお祝いギフト。同時に祝賀会のプロデュースの依頼を促すのが狙い。2方向に開く箱には、紙吹雪、ろうそく、ハッピーバースデーを奏でるオルゴール等が入っている。

S: SONO   CL: Emotion Builders   CD: Alejandro de Montagut   AD: Ruben Ibanez

138

Others

1
Relocation announcement that uses a building motif
This is an announcement of the office relocation of Cross World Connections, which produces and supports creators. The card is in the shape of a building and was designed to be three-dimensional with cut out portions.

クリエイターをプロデュース、サポートするエージェントの移転通知
クリエイターをプロデュース、サポートするクロスワールドコネクションズのオフィス移転の通知。建物の形をモチーフとした形状や型抜きにより、立体感のあるカードに仕上がっている。

CL, S: Cross World Connections   CD: Junko Wong   AD: Creative Team Junie Moon

2
Wedding reception invitation
This is an invitation card for a wedding reception. Stressing fun and impact, the invitation boldly incorporates a photo of the bride and groom into the design. The couple also found it amusing.

新郎新婦のイラストが大胆にとびだす結婚パーティー招待状
結婚パーティーのインビテーション・カード。楽しさ、インパクトを重視し、新郎新婦の写真を大胆に使用したデザインに。本人たちも笑ってくれた。

DF, S: GWG inc.   CL: RJB & MOMO   CD, AD, D: Akihiro Ikegoshi   I: Rockin' Jelly Bean

Others

Office relocation announcement expressing company growth using squares
A notice to inform recipients that Spicers Paper, a company that deals in paper products, was moving to larger quarters. Square die-cut windows become gradually larger, conveying the idea of the company's growth, and when the notice is folded the word "larger" appears by itself.

徐々に大きくなる四角形が成長を表す、紙メーカーのオフィス移転案内
紙を専門とするSpicers Paperがより大きな場所に移転したことを知らせる案内。徐々に大きくなる型抜きの正方形は成長を表し、折り曲げると、「larger（より大きく）」という言葉が現れる。

DF, S: Giorgio Davanzo Design   CL: Spicers Paper   D: Giorgio Davanzo

Others

1

Birth announcement that conveys the pleasure of a new arrival
Personal message to announce the arrival of a new member of the family. The card itself becomes a square when it is folded. Glossy paper is used. The newborn baby is a girl and the announcement comes with a CD of Stevie Wonder's "Isn't She Lovely".

子どもが生まれた喜びを伝えるCD付き挨拶状
新しい家族ができたことを知らせるパーソナルな挨拶状。2つ折りにすると正方形になるカードには、光沢のある紙を使用。女児なので、スティービー・ワンダーが愛娘のために作った曲「Isn't She Lovely」のCDを付けた。

DF, S: CASE CL: VERHOEVEN / DIRKS AD: Kees Wagenaars

Relocation announcement for TEL DESIGN studio
This notice announces the company's move to Rotterdam. Part of the map can be cut out. "Lekker belangrijk" (meaning: very important) is expressed in a sardonically different way to mean the opposite: "It doesn't matter".

デザイン・スタジオ TEL DESIGN の引越しのお知らせ
ロッテルダムに移転したことを知らせる案内。地図の部分を切り取ることができる。「Lekker belangrijk（直訳：すごく重要）」は「どうでもいいよ」と言いたいときに皮肉で逆の言い方をするオランダの表現。

S: TELDESIGN CD, CW: Jaco Emmen AD: Katinka Hormes P: Javier Velazquez

141

Others

Wedding invitation that includes a display pinwheel
An interactive invitation card produced for a good friend. The theme "learn to fly" was the client's idea. Two pieces of paper that become the wings of a pinwheel represent the bride and the groom. Invited guests bring the assembled pinwheel to the wedding venue and use them as part of the decoration.

組み立て式かざぐるまが式場のディスプレイにもなる結婚式の招待状
親友のために制作したインタラクティブな招待状。テーマの「Learn to fly」は依頼主のアイデア。風車の羽となる2枚の紙は新郎・新婦を表す。完成品を持参してもらい、式場のデコレーションとした。

S: Kurt Dornig Graphikdesign & Illustration   CL: Karin Guldenschuh   CL, D: Gerhard Vonach
AD: Kurt Dornig   D: Katharina Weber

Others

Relocation announcement expressing business expansion and corporate logo using rubber bands

Boxes of rubber bands, a common office supply, are used to symbolize the idea of "moving due to business expansion". The aim is to have an impact on recipients through the use of two interlinked orange circles, which is the company logo.

輪ゴムにより、企業ロゴと事業の「伸び」を表現した引越しのお知らせ

定番オフィス用品のひとつ「輪ゴム」の箱を採用することで、「事業の拡張による引越し」を強調している。企業ロゴである2つ連なるオレンジ色の輪を人々に強く印象付けることを狙った。

CL, S: Circle Communications Ltd.   CD, CW: Irene Fung   CD, AD, D: Lily Tse

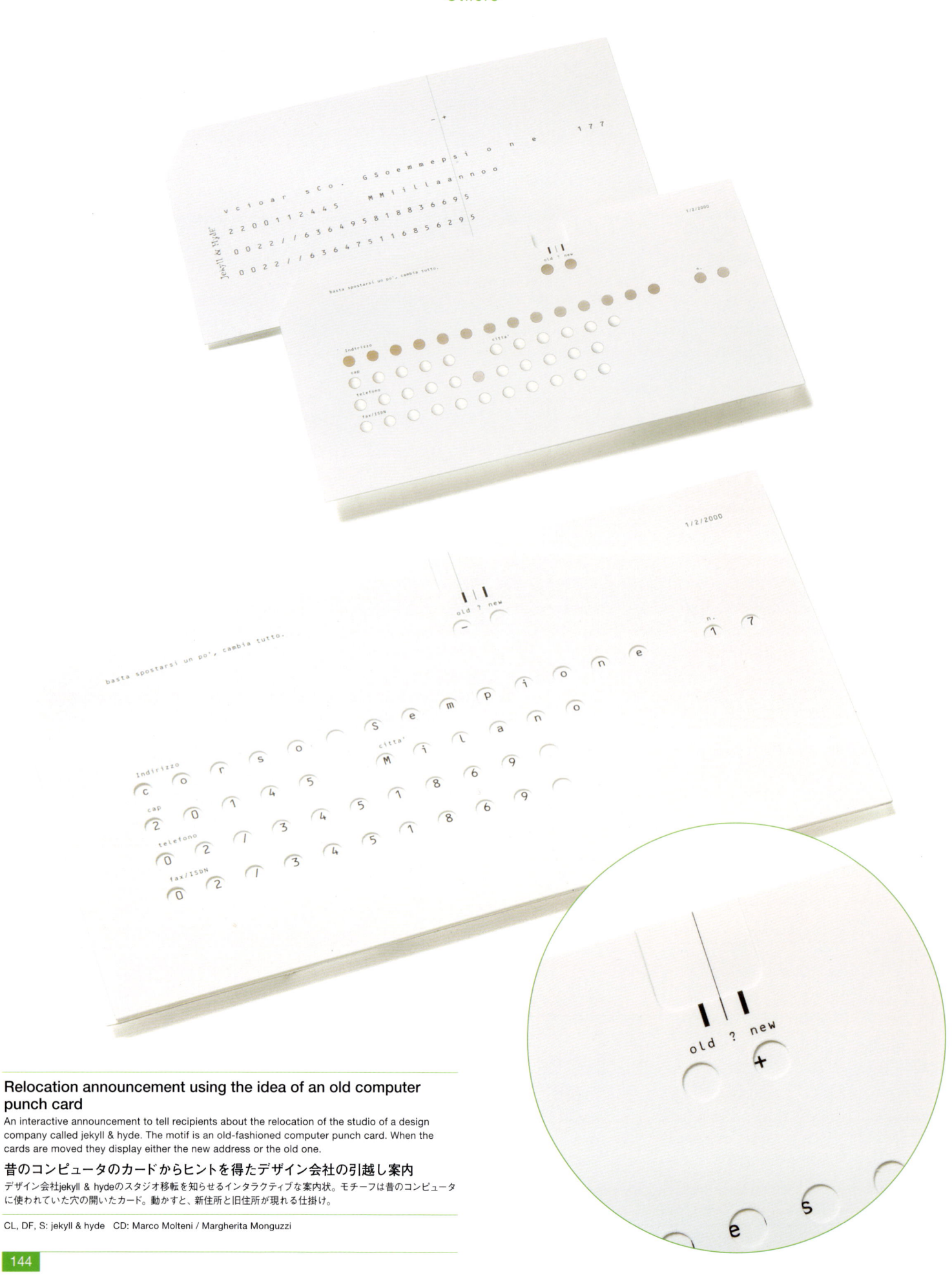

Others

Relocation announcement using the idea of an old computer punch card
An interactive announcement to tell recipients about the relocation of the studio of a design company called jekyll & hyde. The motif is an old-fashioned computer punch card. When the cards are moved they display either the new address or the old one.

昔のコンピュータのカードからヒントを得たデザイン会社の引越し案内
デザイン会社jekyll & hydeのスタジオ移転を知らせるインタラクティブな案内状。モチーフは昔のコンピュータに使われていた穴の開いたカード。動かすと、新住所と旧住所が現れる仕掛け。

CL, DF, S: jekyll & hyde   CD: Marco Molteni / Margherita Monguzzi

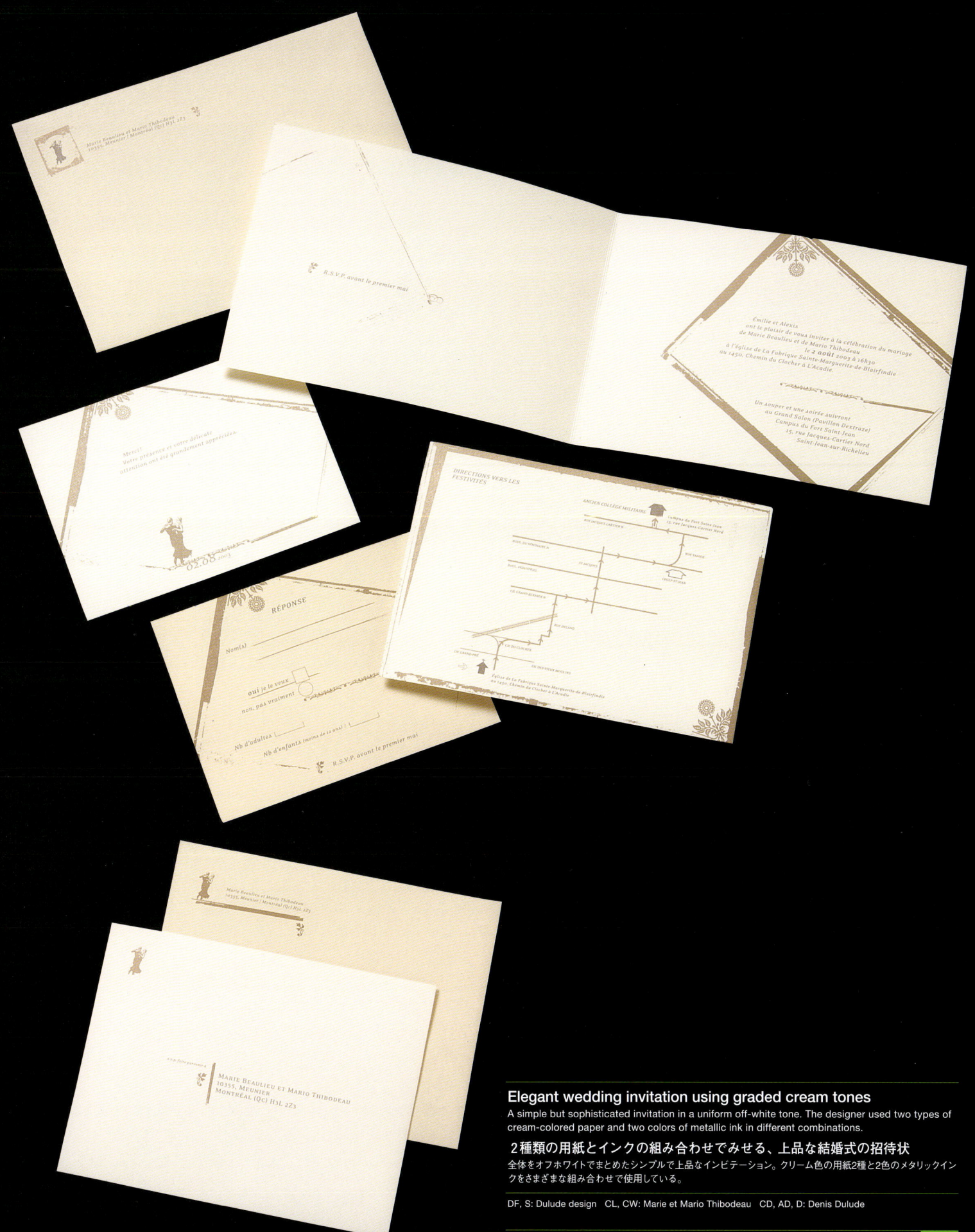

Others

Elegant wedding invitation using graded cream tones
A simple but sophisticated invitation in a uniform off-white tone. The designer used two types of cream-colored paper and two colors of metallic ink in different combinations.

2種類の用紙とインクの組み合わせでみせる、上品な結婚式の招待状
全体をオフホワイトでまとめたシンプルで上品なインビテーション。クリーム色の用紙2種と2色のメタリックインクをさまざまな組み合わせで使用している。

DF, S: Dulude design　CL, CW: Marie et Mario Thibodeau　CD, AD, D: Denis Dulude

145

Others

1
Wedding announcement expressing the idea of two people connected forever
The word "Coccole" written on the side of a container means "to cuddle". This is a play on the name of the famous glue-maker Coccoina. Beneath the inner covering, which contains information about the wedding, there is actual glue, representing the idea that the married couple will stick together forever.

有名な糊の缶をモチーフに「永遠にくっつく」2人を表現した結婚式の案内
容器の側面に書かれたCoccoleとは「抱擁」という意味で、有名な糊メーカーCoccoinaのパロディ。情報が書かれた内蓋の下には実際に糊が入っており、二人が永遠にくっ付くという意味が込められている。

DF, S: Cacao Design　CL: Vittorio and Federica　CD: Mauro Pastore / Masa Magnoni
CD, D: Alessandro Floridia

Wedding invitation designed as an illustrated children's book
An interactive invitation. When the receiver turned the serrated wheels on the sides of the invitation card, he or she could see text and pictures through the die-cut windows on the illustrated cover.

子どもの絵本のような仕掛けがかわいらしいウエディング・インビテーション
インタラクティブな招待状。カードの内側に取り付けられたふたつの歯車を回すと、イラストを施した表紙に型抜きされた穴から、文字やイラストが見える仕組み。

DF, S: Cacao Design　CL: Luca and Sabrina　CD: Mauro Pastore / Masa Magnoni / Alessandro Floridia
D: Giulia Landini

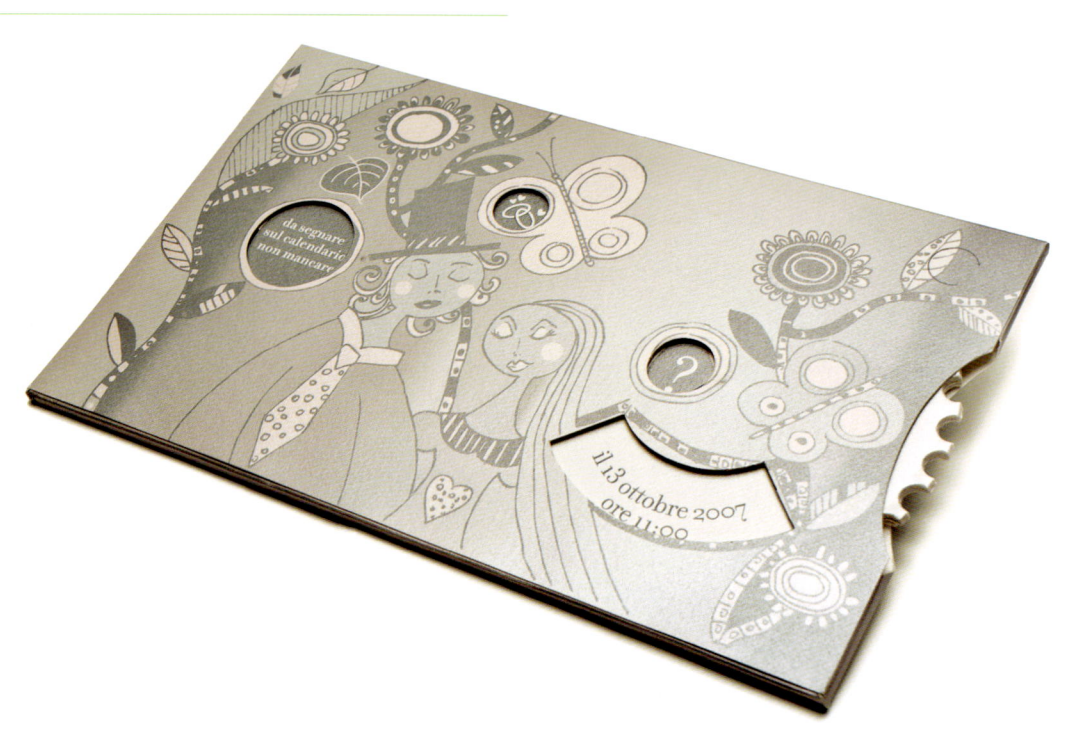

2

146

Others

Chic wedding announcement that coordinates copper color and autumn scenery

The invitations are copper-colored for an autumn theme. Handmade metallic paper is placed on high quality vellum stamped with copper foil and then rolled up and tied with an organdy ribbon. The enclosed leaves are also made of copper, and cinnamon sticks are attached to the top of the invitations.

秋をテーマに銅色でまとめたシックなウエディング案内

秋をテーマに銅色でまとめた招待状。手製のメタリックペーパーと銅の箔押しを施した上質皮紙を重ねて丸め、オーガンジーのリボンを結んだ。同封された葉っぱも銅製、カード上部の棒はシナモンスティックを使用。

S: LL Design   CL: Diane Haddock   CD, AD, D: Lisa Leonard-Koger

Others

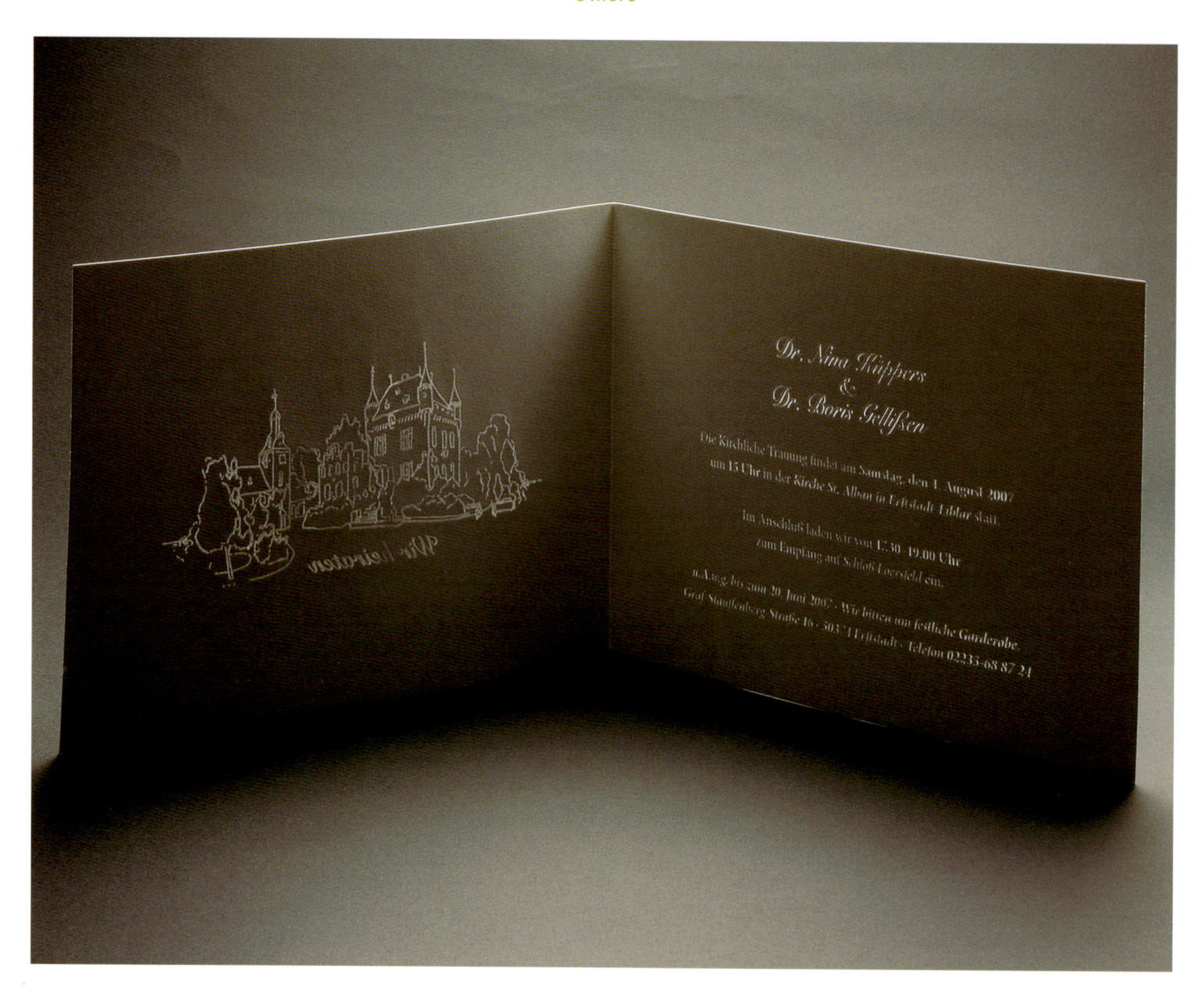

Pure white invitation using a delicate watermark process
The invitation cards have a pleasant texture thanks to an advanced process that uses Haptik, a type of paper ordered from Takeo in Japan. The rice grains are enclose to convey the idea of rice thrown at a wedding, an old German custom. The client and the guests loved the invitation, though several people found it difficult to read.

繊細な透かし加工を施した、お城でのウエディングにふさわしい純白の招待状
竹尾の紙HAPTICを日本から取り寄せ、最新加工技術によって触り心地を楽しめるカードに。米粒はドイツの昔ながらの習慣ライスシャワーに由来。依頼主やゲストは気に入ってくれたが、読みにくいとの声もあった。

S: F1RSTDESIGN.COM   CL: Nina Kuppers & Boris Gellissen   CD: Christopher Ledwig
AD, I: Daniel Taubert

Others

Delicate processed birthday card
This birthday card creates a beautiful world through the use of holographic foil applied to PET material. The card stands up and therefore it can be appreciated as a display.

ホログラム箔により、おとぎ話のような世界観を表現したバースデーカード
ペットボトルで使われているポリエステルの素材にホログラム箔を押し、クリアで美しい世界観を演出したバースデー・カード。スタンド式の構造により、飾って楽しめるようになっている。

S: ART PRINT JAPAN Co.,Ltd.　CD, AD, D: Asuka Nozawa

Others

Invitations to a 25th wedding anniversary party
Invitations to a "lingerie shower" where female friends give gifts of underwear to the wife. The invitations are enclosed in a stitched-paper corset decorated with lace and ribbons. Both the card and the envelope are a type of paper called Curious Metallic.

結婚25周年を祝してランジェリーを贈るパーティーへのコルセット型招待状
女性側に女友達が下着をプレゼントする「ランジェリー・シャワー」への招待状。ステッチが施された素材にレースやリボンをあしらってコルセット型に。カードと封筒にはCurious Metalicという紙を使用。

S: LL Design   CL: Diane Haddock   CD, AD: Lisa Leonard-Koger

1

2

Birthday party invitation for Roberto Valerio
Real knives and forks are attached to the invitation card for an outdoor birthday dinner party. The plastic cutlery was vacuum packed onto the card.

屋外ディナーにちなんでナイフとフォークを付けた誕生パーティーのお知らせ
この誕生会では、屋外でのディナー・パーティーが予定されていたことから、本物のナイフとフォークを付けた立体的なインビテーション・カードに。プラスチック製のカトラリーは真空パックされている。

DF, S: Joseph Rossi srl   CL: Roberto Valerio   D: Graphic First Aid

Others

Announcement of a birth, appreciated in a new way
When browsing through the pages, which are divided into three horizontal parts, the recipient discovers the resemblance between the two parents and their child by mixing and matching portions of the three faces. It's a very playful idea. Semi-transparent material was used for the envelope.

今までと違った楽しみ方ができる子どもの誕生のお知らせ
3等分されたページをぺらぺらめくって父親、母親、赤ちゃんの顔を組み合わせながら、親子の似ているところを発見できるという、遊び心にあふれたブックレット。封筒は半透明の紙を使用している。

S: F1RSTDESIGN.COM　　CL: Dara Ludwig & Florian Steps　　CD, P: Christopher Ledwig

Others

1

Wedding reception invitation that uses the motif of a romantic Hong Kong film
In order to express the character of the clients, a famous romantic Hong Kong movie was used as a motif for their wedding reception. Because the reception was carried out in the Chinese way, red was the theme color. Pearl-finish paper was used to create a feeling of extravagance.

香港の恋愛映画をモチーフにした結婚披露宴へのインビテーション
依頼主のキャラクターを表現するため、香港の有名な恋愛映画を結婚パーティーのモチーフとした。中国の伝統的な披露宴だったためテーマカラーには赤を採用。パールの入った紙を使用し、華やかさを演出している。

DF, S: Nex Branding Design　　CL: Anna Lee & Jason Choy　　CD, AD, D: Joseph Leung　　CW: Jason Choy

Wedding invitation that describes the letter W with a yoga pose
Based on the idea that a marriage won't work without balance and harmony, the letter W for wedding is expressed by a couple in a yoga pose. Printable fabric was used. It was a good gift for the guests.

調和をイメージさせるヨガのポーズで「W」の文字を表した結婚式の招待状
結婚はバランスと調和がなくてはうまくいかない、というアイデアから、ヨガのポーズを用いてウエディングの「W」を表した。印刷ができる布素材を使用。ゲストへのステキなプレゼントにもなった。

DF, S: Nex Branding Design　　CL, CW: Fanny To & Joseph Leung　　CD, AD, D: Joseph Leung

2

Index

CLIENTS LIST

A

Ajuntament De Terrassa   77

Anna Lee & Jason Choy   152

Archer Messori   21

B

BAYCREW'S Co.,Ltd.   91

Bioengineering AG   24, 25, 26

BMW-Group   76

Bravo   72

Bridgetown Printing   87

C

CAP Inc.   126

Cariolato   88, 89, 115, 121

CELUX COMPANY LVJ GROUP K.K.   43, 70

Christopher Ovando David   62

Cinzia Maini   75

Circle Communications Ltd.   104, 105, 143

Cross World Connections   139

D

Dara Ludwig & Florian Steps   151

Davis Agency   129

Des Moines Art Center   85

Des Moines Playhouse   58

DHL Japan   47

Diane Haddock   54, 147, 150

DKNY   39

DOOSUNG PAPER   91

E

Eduard Cehovin   18

Eina, Escola De Disseny i Art   71, 81

Emotion Builders   138

Escapes   137

Estudio Eckert＋Zuniga   117

Estudio Focus   128

Executive Men's Salon DONFUN   34

F

Fanny To & Joseph Leung   152

Florinda   97

Fontegrafica   54, 78, 101

Form   14

Fukuda Kenji Graphic Design   108

G

Georgina Goodman   40

Goethe-Institut   16

GOLDWIN   66

H

HANS SCHWARZ,ALOIS KRACHER,MANFRED KRANKL   69

Happycentro＋Sintetik   122

Heinz Wild Design   110, 111, 112

Huber spa   57

I

Il Gufo Spa   56

INTERCELL AG   34

J

jekyll & hyde   144

JOHNLAWRENCESULLIVAN   67

Joseph Rossi   110, 123, 127, 130, 131

Joven Orozco Design   83

K

Karin Guldenschuh / Gerhard Vonach   142

Krio Trans   100

L

L & KONDO   35

LABCLIP   120

Land Securities   79

Lorgan's The Retro Store   31, 36

Luca and Sabrina   146

Lux Fragil   64, 94

M

marco 500   63, 96

Marie et Mario Thibodeau   145

MATITE GIOVANOTTE   80

MEN'S BIGI Co.,Ltd.   75

MISTER BRICK SRL   20

Motel Inc.   23, 64, 65, 74

N

Nagano Sushi   37

nano·univers   74, 81

Nanzuka Underground / Minimal Tokyo / Gelman Lounge   60

Netz fur Kinder   82

New York, NY   15, 55

Nikon   22, 32

Nina Kuppers & Boris Gellissen   148

nordea   48, 68

O

OL3   103

Ono Luce   57

P

Padoan Vernici   121

Palazzo Biscotto / Paterlini Real Estate   19

Pave   28

Pedrho   30

Q

QOR   50

R

Real Art Design Group,Inc.   10, 12, 84

RENE SCHERR   27

Reptile's House   68, 98

RGR   87

RH milano   76

Rimmel / Tribu   52

RJB & MOMO   139

Roberto Valerio   115, 132, 150

S

Santiago Uribe   136

SCANDINAVIAN DESIGNLAB   113

SHAMAN hair   38

SINV   89, 126, 127

Smeg Italy   13

Spicers Paper   140

Surgery Public Relations   61

T

TÊTE HOMME CO.,LTD.   42

The Brand Distillery   72

The Museum of Modern Art   116, 119, 120

The New Zealand Cheese School   48

The Pressley family   86

Tin Tab   45

tinta en lata   107

Tribu   53, 102

Tsuki no Kakera   92

U

Universitat de València   106

UTILITY 33

V

VERHOEVEN / DIRKS   141

Vittorio and Federica   146

VTech Electronics   29

W

Wildwood Hills Ranch   86

WINE & PARTNERS   90

WORLD CO.,LTD.   41, 44

X

Xose Teiga   17

Z

Zadig & Voltaire   59, 73

804©GRAPHIC DESIGN   109

SUBMITTORS LIST

A

alessandridesign
Austria   34, 69, 90

Alexander Gelman
USA / Japan   60

Aloof Design
United Kingdom   40, 45, 72

antenna graphic base
Japan   75

ART PRINT JAPAN Co.,Ltd.
Japan   124, 125, 149

B

BAYCREW'S Co.,Ltd.
Japan   91

Brighten the Corners
United Kingdom   16

C

Cacao Design
Italy   50, 52, 53, 54, 78, 101, 102, 103, 146

CAP Inc.
Japan   43, 70, 126

CASE
Netherlands   141

ceft and company
USA   15, 55

CHANTO CO.,LTD.
Japan   51

CIPS CO.,LTD.
Japan   98

Circle Communications Ltd.
Hong Kong   104, 105, 143

Cross World Connections
Japan   139

D

Daniela Vascellari
Italy   20, 56

DESIGN BOY Inc.
Japan   41, 44

DESIGN CENTER LTD.
Slovenia   18

Design Unit RE・Bean
Japan   92

DHL Japan
Japan   47

Dotzero Design
USA   87, 129

Dulude design
Canada   145

E

Eina, Escola De Disseny i Art
Spain   71, 81

Espirelius CB
Spain   106

Estudio Eckert＋Zuniga
Spain   117

F

F1RSTDESIGN.COM
Germany   148, 151

Fenice Pool
Italy   13, 21

Form
United Kingdom   14

Fuji-san Graphics
Japan   38

Fukuda Kenji Graphic Design
Japan   33, 108, 137

G

Giorgio Davanzo Design
USA   140

GWG inc.
Japan   139

H

Happycentro＋Sintetik
Italy   30, 72, 122

Heinz Wild Design
Switzerland   24, 25, 26, 110, 111, 112

Hiromi Fujita
Japan   42

Hisashi Narita
Japan   71

J

jekyll & hyde
Italy   68, 76, 98, 144

Joseph Rossi srl
Italy   39, 57, 75, 87, 88, 89, 110, 115, 121, 123, 126, 127, 130, 131, 132, 150

Joven Orozco Design
USA   83

K

Keisuke Unosawa
Japan   116, 119, 120

Kinetic Singapore
Singapore   28, 31, 36, 37

kirameki inc.
Japan   104, 114, 134

KURI-LAB.
Japan   34

Kurt Dornig Graphikdesign & Illustration
Austria   82, 142

L

Links Co.,Ltd.
Japan   46

LL Design
USA   54, 86, 147, 150

Lluc Massaguer Busqueta
Spain   77

M

MATITE GIOVANOTTE
Italy   80

Mirko Ilic Corp
USA   22, 32

N

Nesco
Japan   23, 59, 64, 65, 66, 67, 73, 74, 81

Nex Branding Design
Hong Kong   152

O

Oktober Kommunikationsdesign GmbH
Germany   76

ONE STROKE Co.,Ltd.
Japan   91

orlando facioli design
Brasil   63, 96

P

Paula Rosa
Spain   97

R

Raineri Design
Italy   19, 100

Raquel Quevedo
Spain   62

Real Art Design Group,Inc.
USA   10, 12, 29, 84

RMAC Brand Design
Portugal   64, 94

Roberto Trevino Design
Spain   128, 136

room corporation
Italy   48, 68

S

SAGENVIER DESIGNKOMMUNIKATION
Austria   27

Sayles Graphic Design
USA   58, 85, 86

SCANDINAVIAN DESIGNLAB
Denmark   113

SHIMAMURA TOKYO CORPORATION
Japan   92, 93

SONO
Spain   138

Studio 6.3 and Zulver & Co
United Kingdom   79

STUDIO DESIGN · K CO.,LTD.
Japan   35

Studio Grafico Fez s.n.c
Italy   121

SUN-AD CO.,LTD.
Japan   120

T

TELDESIGN
Netherlands   141

That's Nice LLC
USA   33

The Creative Method
Australia   48

Tidbit Co.,Ltd.
Japan   39

tinta en lata
Spain   107

Tupos Design Company
Hong Kong   118

W

Warmrain
United Kingdom   61

X

Xose Teiga
Spain   17

804©GRAPHIC DESIGN
Germany   109

パワーDM
Creative Card Design:Promotional Greetings

Art Director: Akiko Shiba　　アートディレクター: 柴 亜季子
Designer: Kazuo Abe　　デザイナー: 阿部かずお
Editor: Yasuhiro Sekimoto　　編集: 関本康弘
Photographer: Kuniharu Fujimoto　　写真: 藤本邦治
Translator & Coordinator: Mikiko Shirakura　　翻訳・コーディネーター: 白倉三紀子
Translator: Philip Brasor　　翻訳: フィリップ・ブレイザー
Publisher: Shingo Miyoshi　　発行者: 三芳伸吾

First edition, first issue July 8, 2008
2008年7月8日　初版第1刷発行

Publishing office: PIE BOOKS
発行所: ピエ・ブックス

2-32-4, Minami-Otsuka, Toshima-ku, Tokyo 170-0005 JAPAN
Editor: Phone: ＋81-3-5395-4820　Fax: ＋81-3-5395-4821
e-mail: editor@piebooks.com
Sales: Phone: ＋81-3-5395-4811　Fax: ＋81-3-5395-4812
sales@piebooks.com
http://www.piebooks.com

〒170-0005　東京都豊島区南大塚2-32-4
編集
Tel: 03-5395-4820　Fax: 03-5395-4821
e-mail: editor@piebooks.com
営業
Tel: 03-5395-4811　Fax: 03-5395-4812
e-mail: sales@piebooks.com
http://www.piebooks.com

Printing and binding: Sannichi Printing Co.,Ltd.
印刷・製本　株式会社サンニチ印刷

No part of this publication may be reproduced or utilized in any form
or by any means, including photocopying or quotation,
without prior written permission from PIE BOOKS.
Books with missing or improperly collated pages will be exchanged.

本書の収録内容の無断転載、複写、引用等を禁じます。
落丁、乱丁はお取り替えいたします。

©2008 PIE BOOKS

ISBN978-4-89444-677-9 C3070

Printed in Japan

THE PIE COLLECTION

IN-STORE DISPLAY GRAPHICS
店頭コミュニケーショングラフィックス

Page: 216 (Full Color)　￥14,000+Tax

店頭でのプロモーション展開においては、空間デザインだけでなくグラフィックデザインが果たす役割も重要です。本書では、空間のイメージとグラフィックツールのコンセプトが一貫している作品をはじめ、限られたスペースで有効活用できるディスプレーキットや、P.O.P.の役割も果たすショップツールなどを広く紹介します。

A useful display tool for a limited space, display examples which show the harmonization among packaging, shop interior and in-store promotional graphics, a creative point-of-sale tool which stands out among others. This book is a perfect resource for designers and marketing professionals.

CHARACTER DESIGN TODAY
キャラクターデザイン・トゥデイ

Page: 232 (Full Color)　￥14,000+Tax

キャラクターは企業と消費者とを結ぶ有効なコミュニケーションツールといえます。競合商品との差別化をはかるため、企業のサービスを消費者にわかりやすく伝えるためなど、その役割は様々です。本書では、キャラクターのデザインコンセプト、プロフィールとともに広告やツールの展開例を収録。巻頭では、キャラクターが決定するまでの過程やボツ案を特集し、長く愛されるキャラクターをデザインするポイントを探ります。

200 successful characters with each profile, concept as well as the graphic examples. A featured article about the process of creating a character from scratch is also included with useful examples.

PACKAGE FORM AND DESIGN
ペーパーパッケージデザイン大全集　作例＆展開図(CD-ROM付)

Page: 240 (Full Color)　￥7,800+Tax

大好評の折り方シリーズ第3弾。製品を守りブランドアイデンティティーのアピールとなるパッケージ。本書ではバラエティーに富んだかたちのペーパーパッケージ約200点を国内外から集め、その作例と展開図を紹介していきます。展開図を掲載したCD-ROM付きでクリエイターやパッケージ制作に関わる人たちの参考資料として永久保存版の1冊です。

This is the third title focusing on paper packaging in "Encyclopedia of Paper Folding Design" series. The 150 high quality works are all created by the industry professionals; the perfect shapes and beautiful designs are practical and yet artistic. The template files in pdf file on CD-ROM.

DESIGN IDEAS FOR RENEWAL
再生グラフィックス

Page: 240 (Full Color)　￥14,000+Tax

本書では"再生"をキーワードにデザインの力で既存の商業地や施設、ブランドを甦らせた事例を特集します。リニューアル後のグラフィックツールを中心に、デザインコンセプトや再生後の効果についても紹介します。企業や地域の魅力を再活性させるためにデザインが果たした役割を実感できる1冊です。

A collection of case studies - with "regeneration" and "renewal" as their keywords - showing commercial districts, facilities and brands brought back to life through the power of design. Focusing on mainly the post-renovation graphic tools, we present the design concepts and their regenerative effects through which readers will see the role that design can play in reigniting the allure of companies and communities.

GIRLY GRAPHICS
ガーリー グラフィックス

Page: 200 (Full Color)　￥9,800+Tax

"ガーリー"とは女の子らしさの見直しや、ポップでありながらもキュートといった、女の子らしさを楽しむポジティブな姿勢を意味します。そんな"ガーリー"な空気感を、ポスター・DM・カタログ・パッケージなどのデザイン領域で、魅力的に表現した作品を紹介します。

A word "girly" represents an expression of reconstructing positive images about being girls. Today, those powerful and contagious "girly" images with great impact successfully grab attentions not only from girls but also from a broad range of audience. This book features about those 300 enchanted and fascinated advertisements such as posters, catalogs, shop cards, business cards, books, CD jackets, greeting cards, letterheads, product packages and more.

NEO JAPANESQUE DESIGN
ネオ ジャパネスク デザイン

Page: 224 (Full Color)　￥14,000+Tax

2006年2月に発刊し好評を得た「ネオ ジャパネスク グラフィックス」。待望の第二弾「ネオ ジャパネスク デザイン」がいよいよ登場。ショップイメージ・ロゴ＆マークのカテゴリが新たに加わり、内容・クオリティともにバージョンアップした"和"デザインの最前線を紹介します。

This is the sister edition to "Neo Japanesque Graphics" published in 2006, and this new book includes even more modern yet Japanese taste designs which will give creative professionals inspirational ideas for their projects. Among various graphic works, this second title features shop design such as restaurants, bars and hotels, also features a variety of Japanese logos.

文字を読ませる広告デザイン 2

Page: 192 (Full Color)　￥9,800+Tax

パッと見た時に文字が目に入ってきて、しかも読みやすいデザインの広告物やパッケージの特集です。優れたデザインや文字組み、コピーによって見る側に文字・文章を読ませることを第一に考えられた広告を厳選します。ポスター、新聞広告、チラシ、車内吊り、雑誌広告、DM、カタログ、パンフレット、本の装丁、パッケージ、看板・サインなど多岐なジャンルにわたり紹介します。

Sales in Japan only.

FASHION BRAND GRAPHICS
ファッション グラフィックス

Page: 160 (Full Color)　￥7,800+Tax

本書は、ファッション、アパレルにおけるグラフィックデザインに力を入れた販促ツールを、厳選して紹介します。通常のショップツールはもちろん、シーズンごと、キャンペーンごとのツールも掲載。激しく移り変わるファッション業界において、お客様を飽きさせない、華やかで魅力的な作品を凝縮した1冊です。

The fashion brands that appear in this collection are among the most highly regarded in Japan and herein we introduce some of their commonly used marketing tools including catalogues, shopping cards and shopping bags, together with their seasonal promotional tools and novelties. This publication serves for not only graphic designers, but also people in the fashion industry, marketing professionals.

THE PIE COLLECTION

GRAPHIC SIMPLICITY
シンプル グラフィックス

Page: 248 (Full Color)　￥14,000+Tax

上質でシンプルなデザイン — 見た目がすっきりとして美しいのはもちろんのこと、シンプルなのに個性的な作品、カラフルなのに上品な作品、フォントやロゴがさりげなく効いている作品など、その洗練されたデザインは見る人を魅了してやみません。本書は厳選された作品を国内外から集め、落ち着いた大人の雰囲気にまとめ上げた本物志向のグラフィックコレクションです。

Simple, high-quality design work: not just crisply elegant and eye catching, but uncluttered yet distinctive, colorful yet refined, making subtly effective use of fonts and logos; in short, sophisticated design that seduces all who sees it.

BEST FLYER 365DAYS NEWSPAPER INSERT EDITION
ベストチラシ 365 デイズ　折込チラシ編

Page: 256 (Full Color)　￥14,000+Tax

一番身近な広告媒体である新聞の折込チラシ。地域に密着したお得な情報を提供するものから、セレブ＆クールで夢のようなビジュアルのものまで多種多様です。本書では、1年間（365日）の各セールスシーズンでまとめたものから、1枚だけで効果的に商品をPRしたチラシまで、優れたデザインの旬な折込チラシ800点を収録しています。広告の制作に携わる人びとに必携のデザインサンプル集です。

This book contains many examples of excellently designed, topical flyers, ranging from seasonal advertisements to flyers for a single product. It is an anthology of design samples for creative professionals in the advertising industry.

1&2 COLOR EDITORIAL DESIGN
1・2色でみせるエディトリアルデザイン

Page: 160 (Full Color)　￥7,800+Tax

少ない色数でエディトリアルデザインする際には、写真の表現や本文使用色に制限がある分、レイアウトや使用する紙に工夫や表現力が問われます。本書は1色、2色で魅力的にレイアウトされた作品を、インクや用紙データのスペックと併せて紹介します。

This book presents many of well-selected editorial design examples, featuring unique and outstanding works using one or two colors. All works in this single volume present designers enormous hints for effective and unique techniques with information on specs of inks and papers. Examples include PR pamphlets, magazines, catalogs, company brochures, and books.

BEYOND ADVERTISING: COMMUNICATION DESIGN
コミュニケーション デザイン

Page: 224 (Full Color)　￥15,000+Tax

限られた予算のなか、ターゲットへ確実に届く、費用対効果の高い広告をどのように実現するか？ 今デザイナーには、広告デザインだけでなく、コミュニケーション方法までもデザインすることが求められています。本書では「消費者との新しいコミュニケーションのカタチ」をテーマに実施されたキャンペーンの事例を幅広く紹介。様々なキャンペーンを通して、コミュニケーションを成功させるヒントを探求します。

Reaching the target market a limited budget: how is cost effective promotion achieved? What are the most effective ways to combine print and digital media? What expression reaches the target market? The answers lie in this book, with "new ways and forms of communicating with the consumer" as its concept.

PICTGRAM & ICON GRAPHICS 2
ピクトグラム＆アイコングラフィックス 2

Page: 208 (Full Color)　￥13,000+Tax

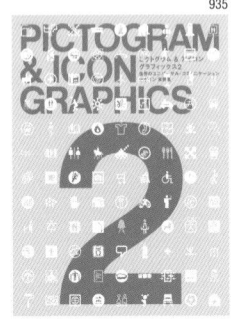

本書では、視覚化に成功した国内・海外のピクトグラムとアイコンを紹介します。空港・鉄道・病院・デパート・動物園といった施設の案内サインとして使用されているピクトグラムやマップ・フロアガイドをはじめ、雑誌やカタログの中で使用されているアイコンなど、身近なグラフィックまでを業種別に掲載。巻末に、一般的によく使われるピクトグラム（トイレ・エスカレーター・駐車場など）の種類別一覧表を収録。

Second volume of the best-seller title "Pictogram and Icon Graphics". Full-loaded with the latest pictograms around the world. Signage, floor guides and maps in airport, railway, hospital, department store, zoo and many more. Contained a wide variety of icons, including those found in catalogs and magazines, etc.

WORLD CALENDAR DESIGN
ワールドカレンダーデザイン

Page: 224 (Full Color)　￥9,800+Tax

本書では国内外のクリエーターから集めたカレンダーを特集します。優れたグラフィックスが楽しめるスタンダードなタイプから、形状のユニークなもの、仕掛けのあるものなど、形状別にカテゴリーに分けて紹介します。カレンダー制作のためのデザインソースとしてはもちろん、ユニークな作品を通じて、様々なグラフィックスに活かせるアイデアが実感できる内容です。

The newest and most distinctive calendars from designers around the world. The collection features a variety of calendar types highly selected from numerous outstanding works ranging from standard wall calendars to unique pieces in form and design, including lift-the flap calendar, 3D calendar, pencil calendar and more.

カタログ・新刊のご案内について

総合カタログ、新刊案内をご希望の方は、はさみ込みのアンケートはがきをご返送いただくか、下記ピエ・ブックスへご連絡下さい。

CATALOGS and INFORMATION ON NEW PUBLICATIONS

If you would like to receive a free copy of our general catalog or details of our new publications, please fill out the enclosed postcard and return it to us by mail or fax.

CATALOGUES ET INFORMATIONS SUR LES NOUVELLES PUBLICATIONS

Si vous désirez recevoir un exemplaire qratuit de notre catalogue généralou des détails sur nos nouvelles publication. veuillez compléter la carte réponse incluse et nous la retourner par courrierou par fax.

CATALOGE und INFORMATIONEN ÜBER NEUE TITLE

Wenn Sie unseren Gesamtkatalog oder Detailinformationen über unsere neuen Titel wünschen.fullen Sie bitte die beigefügte Postkarte aus und schicken Sie sie uns per Post oder Fax.

ピエ・ブックス

〒170-0005　東京都豊島区南大塚2-32-4
TEL: 03-5395-4811　FAX: 03-5395-4812
www.piebooks.com

PIE BOOKS

2-32-4 Minami-Otsuka Toshima-ku Tokyo 170-0005 JAPAN
TEL：+81-3-5395-4811　FAX：+81-3-5395-4812
www.piebooks.com